SUPERDEAL

By the same author

MANAGING NEGOTIATIONS (with John Benson
and John McMillan)
EVERYTHING IS NEGOTIABLE!
NEGOTIATE ANYWHERE!

SUPERDEAL

How to Negotiate Anything!

GAVIN KENNEDY

For Alan
from Heather

[signature]

$$\overline{C}$$

CENTURY PUBLISHING

LONDON   MELBOURNE   AUCKLAND   JOHANNESBURG

For Beatrice

Copyright © Gavin Kennedy 1986
Copyright © cartoons Century Hutchinson
Cartoons by Martin Honeysett

First published in 1986 by Century Hutchinson Ltd,
Brookmount House, 62–65 Chandos Place, Covent Garden,
London WC2N 4NW

Century Hutchinson Publishing Group (Australia) Pty Ltd
16–22 Church Street, Hawthorn, Melbourne, Victoria 3122

Century Hutchinson Group (NZ) Ltd
32–34 View Road, PO Box 40-086, Glenfield, Auckland 10

Century Hutchinson Group (SA) Pty Ltd
PO Box 337, Bergvlei 2012, South Africa

British Library Cataloguing in Publication Data
Kennedy, Gavin
Superdeal: how to negotiate anything!
1. Negotiation
I. Title
158.5   BF637.N4

ISBN 0-7126-1080-4

Set in Linotron Palatino by
Rowland Phototypesetting Ltd,
Bury St Edmunds, Suffolk

Printed in Great Britain by
St Edmundsbury Press, Bury St Edmunds, Suffolk

Contents

Acknowledgements

No book is ever the product of a single person. Many thousands of buyers, sellers, bureaucrats, relatives, friends, diplomats, clerks, strangers and children have indirectly contributed to *Superdeal*. I cannot thank them all, either enough or individually.

Among those individuals I can name, I gratefully acknowledge John Benson of Nabisco for his influence on my thinking about negotiating over many years.

I would also like to thank: Trevor Davis of Skyline, Edinburgh; John McMillan and Stephen White of Scotwork, Glasgow; John Winkler of Winkler Marketing, Brighton; Geoff Lazberger of Abel Computing, Papua New Guinea; Fred Slowick of Washington Speakers Bureau, Alexandria, Virginia; Kris Helgersen of Marine Tech, Oslo; and Ewan McCaig and Stewart Hislop, of the Doric Tavern, Edinburgh.

Professor John Small of Heriot-Watt University kindly allowed me time to complete the manuscript when deadlines began to press. Joan Burnie read and commented on various chapters. Several friends listened to and commented upon numerous expositions of incidents, scenes and dialogue that appear in the text.

My editor, Vivien James, deserves a special thanks for her incredible patience, her gently critical touch and her firm support at all stages of *Superdeal*'s gestation.

As usual, the main burden fell on the family. Patricia and the children suffered my absences with their normal good humour. There ought to be a special award for the families of authors. I'd nominate mine on this occasion for a special commendation.

Preface

This book has been written following many requests from readers of my other books on negotiating to extend the coverage to the kinds of transactions all of us engage in every day. From my mail, and from radio phone-ins, I have no doubt that many people are keen to try for Superdeals, and only need a little push to take on the fixed prices and first offers they get from the people they deal with.

Superdeal aims to help you do better as a negotiator. It does not preach, nor is it written in too serious a style. A sense of humour is a Superdealer's best friend – what a threat can't get for you, a laugh might.

Some people (wrongly) think that negotiating is about slyness and cunning, is somehow disreputable and is barely good manners. True, the issues between parties in conflict can be very serious, even fraught with menace. But the resolution of differences by negotiation is one of the most civilised ways we have to come to agreement on issues that originally divide us.

The people I meet at my negotiating clinics are no different from anybody else. They want to improve their negotiating skills in order to make better deals. They want to find deals that are good for them and for the people they deal with. Superdealers have no need to apologise for their approach, for if more people negotiated their differences instead of using other, often violent alternatives, the world would be the happier for it.

If readers learn to love the haggle, acquire the confidence to have their own preferences considered, and get better deals than they at first thought possible or that the other party first put forward, I will regard *Superdeal* as a success.

Finally, a word to you, the reader. As with my previous books on negotiating, I invite you to write and comment on anything you find in the text that you have found useful or with which you disagree. It is always gratifying to hear from readers who take the trouble to think seriously about what they have read. If you have time, why not drop me a line?

GAVIN KENNEDY
22 Braid Avenue
Edinburgh EH10 6EE
Telex: 72165

Introduction

The population of our world is divided (unequally) into two distinct camps: those who can live within their current incomes, and are quite happy to continue doing so, and those who can't and want to do something about it. If you recognise yourself as a member of the second group, you might be comforted to know that it is by far and away the larger. And if you really want to do something about it, keep reading.

Superdeal is for you if you need to make your income go further, either because you need more than you have or because you want more than you can get. It's not that you are greedy – you just can't live on your income. No matter how rich or poor you are, your income never seems sufficient to buy all that you want and, sometimes, it is not even sufficient to buy all that you need.

There are only two ways that you can reduce the imbalance between your income and your wants: you can either reduce your wants, or you can make your income go further.

Reducing your wants is a consequence of a commitment to the Zen Way to Affluence: human wants should be finite and few! Yes, you too can enjoy an abundance of income in excess of your needs if, *but only if*, you are prepared to suffer a very low standard of living. But the realities of abject poverty, when experienced by those other than cranks, soon undermines the determination of those who wish upon themselves and their families the lifestyle (and life expectancy!) of the Stone Age.

In contrast, Superdealers are more interested in making their incomes go further.

If you want to get more from your income, you can use the proven techniques contained in *Superdeal*. You do not need to be a 'born' haggler, you do not need a Machiavellian mind nor do you need to learn some complicated game-plan. All you have to do is select some simple techniques that work when applied to your lifestyle.

Superdealers *negotiate*. Everybody else pays the price on the tag, or accepts the first thing they are offered. You always have the fundamental choice: accept whatever somebody else thinks is good (or good enough) for you, or set about negotiating a better deal for yourself.

Superdealers do not *always* challenge whatever they are offered, but if you *never* challenge anything at all, if you always meekly accept what is on offer, you are accepting a lower living standard than your current financial circumstances justify. In other words, you can do better if you want or need to – with a Superdeal!

Undoubtedly, sometimes we could make better use of our time than spending it haggling over trivial amounts or issues. There is no need to feel guilty about this – there is much more to life than *permanent* negotiation – but we make what we have go further if we know how to haggle at least some of the time.

Superdeal shows you how to haggle, how to negotiate a better deal when you want to, and when circumstances make it worthwhile, even imperative, that you do so. It demonstrates the ploys that will work for you when you want to use them, and also shows you how to recognise them when somebody else tries them on you (and what you can do about this).

If you can make your current income go 5, 10 or 20 per cent further than it does at present, this has to be a real benefit to you. Superdealing is as good as a pay rise – even better than one when you apply the same techniques to getting more pay (or alimony) as well as making your income go further! The fastest way to increase your living standards is to make what you have at present go further. You need not be resigned to accepting your present lot: losers cringe, winners challenge!

Most people do not like haggling – until, that is, they have tried and found how easy it is to get a better deal. The most self-effacing of people – and bubbling media stars – become blissfully ecstatic after they try for a discount and get one. The pay-off in sheer self-confidence is often worth far more than the actual monetary saving they make, and it is not long before they are looking for another opportunity to do themselves a favour by trying for a haggle.

But even if you have the outlook of a Zen evangelist and the patience of a saint, you still have to deal with other people, and people are not the easiest of creatures to deal with. They have the irritating habit of having ideas, hopes and interests – and not a few demands that they are determined to get – and these can be diametrically opposed to what we want or what we can offer.

As with cash deals, people deals are not always possible, given your current circumstances, the time that you have available, the amount of bother that you are willing to endure and the history of what you have endured already. But if a better alternative to what is on offer is obtainable by negotiation, you owe it to yourself to know how to go about getting a better deal than the one chosen for you by the other person.

Superdeal's simple, yet powerful, techniques for winning will help you make your money go further and your personal relationships to become a little less fraught – and that has to be better for all concerned.

Like everybody else, Superdealers experience a few disappointments, some frustrations and the occasional dose of humility. Unlike everybody else, Superdealers believe, and practise, the dictum: Those that can, do, and those who can't can learn to do better!

I know of no more enjoyable way to get more of what you want than by applying the techniques of *Superdeal*. However, if circumstances suggest alternative techniques to those in *Superdeal*, go ahead and try them. If my advice does not appear to be right for you, try somebody else's or, better still, follow your own instincts, but always make a note of what happened – what went right, what went wrong – for future reference. Use *Superdeal* as your starting point. If you see or hear of a tip that works for you – or contradicts a message in *Superdeal* – add your own notes to mine (and write and tell me about it).

Just remember, no matter what you are offered by somebody else, you may be able to move towards a better deal simply by saying: 'On the other hand, we could do it this way . . .'

1

You don't have to join 'em

There is no more lonely time and place than a High Street emporium a few minutes before you try for a discount. Everything in the retail business – the layout, the design, the way the staff approach you, the presence of other customers, the presentation of the merchandise, the pat lines of sellers, the printed price tags, the expectation that you will buy it their way – has only one purpose: to intimidate you into paying the price on the tag.

Bucking the system, asking for a better deal than the one they offer, in short, haggling, is discouraged as 'unBritish', or troublesome, or both. Hence, most people don't. They take the tag price.

Little Oliver Twist knew all about the loneliness of that walk to the counter to ask for more than he was first offered. But he did it! And so can you.

Unlike poor Oliver, you are not a supplicant. You have nothing to fear when challenging somebody trying to sell you something. You are their equal! Without you, and the millions like you, shops would go out of business. When they can't sell their goods at the prices they first thought of, they hold a 'sale' and offer them at a discount. Who says you must wait for a sale before you can do better than the price on the tag?

To help you take those first few steps to a Superdeal we shall look at the selling business, the behaviour of sellers, their ploys and dodges, and how you can cope with them once you understand what they are trained to do to you.

The message is: you don't have to join the majority of customers who do what is expected of them; Superdealers have an alternative.

Economics in one lesson

It is the first law of economics (and of *affaires de coeur*) that there is no such thing as a free lunch, because someone, somewhere, pays for it, but there is no law in economics (and perhaps in *affaires de coeur*) that says that the someone who pays should be you!

Assuming that you do not have access to a bottomless pit out of which you can draw unlimited funds, whatever you spend on cakes cannot simultaneously be spent on ale. You have to choose how to spend *each* pound, for you can't spend the *same* pound twice.

Hence, you must choose: wanting to spend more than you have (the common condition of the human race, saints included), you must either spend more wisely or wisely acquire more to spend. The latter is more difficult than spending more wisely, if only because it is easier to get better deals while spending your money, than it is to persuade somebody else to give you more money to spend. (If this is untrue for you, embrace your 'bottomless pit'.)

If you can buy a fridge for £100 instead of £120, you save £20. Will that £20 gather dust in your purse or is there something else that you could spend it on? What are you giving up if you pay £3000 more than you needed to for your house? Are you so affluent that £3000 – or £30,000 – is of no consequence? If you could save £5 on a £20 purchase, would you be embarrassed with the £5 change?

Reduce your monthly expenditure and your income will go further, because you can then choose to buy additional goods (food, wine, clothes, toys) and services (holidays, insurance, concerts), or to run down your debts or invest in a savings account.

You need a strategy for minimising the amount you spend on individual items so that you have more left over to spend on other things. *Superdeal* gives you that strategy.

Starting over

Whatever else stays the same, this is the last day you will accept other people's decisions and choices: you are going to decide and choose for yourself.

First, you must purge yourself of any delusions that you owe latter-day Sheriffs of Nottingham a living ('rob the poor, feed the rich'), or owe modern Robin Hoods a donation ('rob the rich, feed the poor'). It's not that you are against anybody getting richer; nor are you in favour of anybody getting poorer. It's just that you are fed up with being a victim – if the Sheriffs of Nottingham aren't ripping you off at one end, the Robin Hoods are taxing you at the other. This is precisely what will happen as long as you spend your hard-earned income at prices the sellers choose for you, and shun the financial independence that keeps you ahead of the tax ambitions of politicians.

From now on, however, you will negotiate before you pay for anything. In sum, you will make sure that you 'get something back' off the price *they* first quote – that is, you aim to get other people to improve on their first offer.

To analyse what you will *not* be doing once you become a Superdealer, let's start with a typical purchase. Think of something you bought very recently, or go out and buy something right now. It doesn't matter what it is, or why you want it. The bigger the item the better, because (hopefully!) this is the last time you will buy anything the way you normally do.

Recent practice is better than memory, so go out now and buy something for the house (some furniture, a teapot, a fridge, a new carpet, etc.), or something for yourself (some clothes or a case of wine). Buy the item the way you normally do, i.e. pay the seller the asking price without any attempt to get a discount or any other concession on the terms they impose as they take your money.

Now that you've got your new possession home, and you are admiring it with that degree of self-satisfaction reserved for cats that get the cream, how do you feel?

Great?

You're kidding! If you feel great, you need a crash course in being humble, because you have just done what 97 per cent of the population do *all* the time – they pay the price on the tag and accept whatever the seller imposes without resistance.

Alternatively, you might feel *lousy*. That's better because, unless you feel lousy about paying the asking price, you'll never want to make your income go further. Remember when you decided to buy the item you last purchased? You could well have felt euphoric – we often feel euphoric when we decide to buy something, for it shows, if on'ʒ privately, that we can buy what we want – but how did you feel about what you paid for whatever it was that caught your fancy? Never mind for the moment *why* you paid their price, you can still separate yourself from the gullible majority who submit to the 'fixed'-price, take-it-or-leave-it system.

How did you go about buying?

If the seller mentioned the price, it would only be in response to a direct question ('How much is this wotsit, please?'), and you can bet yourself a free dinner at the Savoy that, having read off the price on the tag, the seller went as quiet as a mute in a vacuum. After all, having announced the price, what more had he or she to say? You either take the item at that price or leave it.

Most buyers pay the price on the tags. If, in a forlorn hope that you will be offered a discount, you moan about it being 'expensive', etc., you seldom – very seldom! – go a step further and directly ask for a reduction, and if you do, even the dumbest (particularly the dumbest!) sales assistant knows that you are likely to accept any excuse in place of a definite 'no' for an answer.

The lesson is simple: you pay more for whatever you buy than you need to. Knowing this, the conclusion is as compelling as it is obvious: you must commit yourself right now never to do the same thing again.

The 100 per cent discount

The first thing you must do before you purchase an item is to *decide why you want it in the first place*.

The world's biggest discounts come from *not* buying something in the first place – that way you can save 100 per cent! If you can eliminate impulse purchases, you will save yourself a lot of money in a short time, and even more over the long haul.

Sellers employ the world's most expensive psychologists (that's why they are so expensive!) to advise them on setting impulse traps for people with money to spend. You are walking by a store window or a shop counter or are quietly reading the Sunday supplement, and – *bingo!* – the package, the product, the layout and the association of ideas all come together and you buy.

You can't help yourself. Psychologists have seen inside your head and got your number.

You spend your money without thinking about it. Regret might come later, though it is likely you will blame yourself, not the seller, and, as likely, you will rationalise your behaviour: 'I just had to buy it'; 'I've always wanted one'; 'It will come in handy when we go on holiday'; 'It was so pretty, I couldn't stop myself'; 'At that price, I would have been a fool to let it go', etc.

By thinking beforehand about your reasons for buying, and *only buying when you have thought beforehand about your reasons*, you stem the haemorrhage of your cash caused by impulse buying. An impulse buy can always be distinguished from a planned buy: when did you think about your reasons for buying? *Before* you saw the product (a planned buy) or after you saw the product (an impulse buy)?

When you utter the immortal line, 'I'll think about it,' every seller within earshot has a collapse of the spirit as total as someone who wakes up and realises they were only dreaming that Tina Turner/Robert Redford said 'yes'. Why? Because, ninety-nine times out of a hundred, someone who says they'll think about it, doesn't. Sellers know that, if they let you out of their sight, they are likely not to see you within it again. And you know that, if you think about it, the biggest saving comes from not buying at all.

The sizzle ploy

Reasons for a purchase that are related to *facts* ('I need the cupboard to store my cups') are more powerful for your negotiations with a seller than reasons related to *moods* and *emotions* ('That dresser looks fantastic').

Why? Because it's more difficult to improve a deal when your moods or emotions rather than factual reasons motivate your purchase.

It is easier to convince yourself that the cupboard is too expensive for your factual needs ('£600 to store my cups!') than it is when you are striving to satisfy an emotional need ('Only £600 for such a beautiful antique farmhouse dresser?'). Because emotions, like the weather, change every moment while needs change more

'THE LADY NEXT DOOR HAS JUST BOUGHT ANOTHER TWO'

slowly, you will regret an emotional purchase sooner than one based on factual reasoning.

Sellers know this, and their psychologists have proved it, and hence they long ago developed a selling technique to ambush you:

Smart sellers selling steak sell the sizzle not the steak.

Get it?

A sizzle appeals to your imagination – that marvellous sizzle as the steak is cooked. It smells good just thinking about it – 'Make that a twelve-ouncer, medium rare, with a side order of a runny egg and some chips. And don't forget the mustard.'

Sizzle selling is not just confined to steaks. For example, sellers of vegetarian food appeal to your desire for good health, or to any compassion you may feel towards dead animals. If sellers can build a selling sequence using the 'sizzle' in a product, supported by marketing aids and advertising, then they are more than halfway to reaching their sales quota for the week.

It is a fact, attested to by hordes of psychologists and, more convincingly, by people who have become rich by selling, that you buy because of the sizzle far more often than you buy because of hard facts about a product.

And for you, this has to be a warning: if the seller is on his or her strongest ground when you see, feel, smell, imagine or touch (ouch!) that sizzle, it follows that you are on your weakest ground, and like a fish about to bite the bait, it's time you shut your mouth and moved over to safer territory.

By becoming immune to sizzle selling, you can better judge if the price the seller wants for the cupboard is too expensive for your needs. If it is (and even if it isn't!), you can argue credibly and with conviction for a discount or some other concession. Alternatively, not knowing your real needs while being inebriated by your moods, you will be less than convincing in an assault on the seller's fanciful price. Just like a dog knows who it is safe to bark at, the seller senses your lack of inner conviction and finds the strength to trot out many fatuous and well-worn excuses for saying 'no'.

Hence, sort out *why* you want the item in question, preferably writing your reasons down. If you feel you are under the influence of a sizzle sale and are very weak on factual reasons for buying the item, reconsider the purchase. Remember, and I'll remind you more than once, you can get a 100 per cent discount by not spending at all!

The tyranny of choice

Before Affluence (B.A.) – the past unknown to anybody under twenty, and forgotten by the rest of us – there was not a great demand for consumer advice. We bought what we and what our parents and grandparents had always bought because the years of wartime rationing and, before that, the depression had preserved consumer choice as a luxury for the very rich. For a long time, it was a laughably inappropriate concept as, for most of us, getting by was more important than buying.

Now, having succumbed to affluence, we have discovered that we need help in making sensible choices. With seventy brands of microwave ovens on sale, which one is worth buying, which ones are lemons? How many video machines can you choose from? What about washing machines, dish washers, toasters, home computers, exercise bikes, vacuum cleaners, loft ladders, twelve-foot dinghies, Teflon cookware, fridges, freezers, shavers, hair driers, Spanish villas, wines, barbecue kits, greenhouses, lawn-mowers and the rest of the badges of consumerism?

One thing is certain: you won't be able to properly research the market and make a considered judgement during the five min-utes it takes you to walk into a store and attract the attention of staff in the shop's display area.

It is a sound general principle that you should study the available products that meet some need you have discovered before you decide on a purchase. To make a sensible purchase, therefore, *you must survey what is available on the market that can meet your needs*.

This will take some time, and for good reason. The more time that you have, the better you will be able to answer the following questions:

- What is available to meet my needs?
- How do the available products differ?
- Do these differences matter to my needs?
- How wide is the price range for this product?
- What reports have been published, either in specialist maga-zines or in the general media, about each product's perform-ance and each company's record for after-sales service?
- What is the second-hand market like for these products?

You can survey the market far more intensely if you take your time. If you are in a hurry, the general rule that 'rushed buys are bad buys' applies.

Your research might reveal that you have various options available, and knowing that you have options enhances your negotiating position. To this end, there is nothing wrong with letting the seller know that you are aware of your options and that you are willing to pursue them if the seller's offer is not good enough. (We shall explore how to do this effectively later.)

It never pays to let the seller know that you cannot be bothered to continue your searches, or to demonstrate that your preparation was less than thorough. They might chase the chance of a maximum price by convincing you that further 'tiresome' searches are unnecessary and hitting you with a 'baffle with waffle' presentation.

Resisting the switch-seller

Thinking out your needs beforehand permits you to discuss credibly the gap (fanciful or real) between your needs and the products *within your price range* that the seller suggests meet those needs.

Few products are priced to be a perfect match for our carefully considered needs, but if one *is* a perfect match and within our price range, there is absolutely no need to disclose this to the seller.

Sellers always attempt to 'switch sell' – that is, move you from a product at the bottom of your price range to another, more expensive one at the top of it:

- You try to buy a basic family saloon car, and the seller tries to move you up to the 'luxury' family saloon range.
- You want a simple music centre that plays records at juke box standard, and the seller tries to switch you to a broadcast-quality quadraphonic system.

This technique is partly an attempt to get you to increase the value of your purchase, but it also has the supplementary objective of confirming your decision to buy the lower-priced version. This last is known as the 'switch' close: your resistance to the switch upwards makes you more determined to stick to the product you can 'afford'. You demand the economy product as a means of stopping further sales patter about the 'expensive' version and, almost with relief, you gladly sign the order to shut the seller up! Naturally, the certainty of your commitment to buy also precludes all but the most determined of you pushing too hard for concessions on the economy version.

It is a fact of business life that sellers make more of an effort to sell products that they believe *partially* meet your needs than they will those that they believe fully meet them.

Why? Because if a product fully meets your disclosed needs, and it is in your disclosed price range, the seller lets the product sell itself. However, all sellers know that an item that is only partially attractive to you will require some additional persuasion on their part before they get a sale.

Hence, by convincing sellers that an item only partially meets your needs, and that you are not going to be switch-sold further up the price range, sellers are more likely to try to induce you to buy an economy version with concessions on the price or in some other area. Thus you get what you want cheaper than you would otherwise.

To this end, **Superdealers never praise the product they are thinking of buying. Instead, they highlight the fact that the product only partially meets their needs, that it is already too expensive** (hence you are immune to switch-selling ploys), **and that to buy anything at all, you will have to be persuaded by some concessions from the seller.**

What do I get for my money?

Do not assume that the price on the tag, or the one mentioned by the seller, is the price that you have to pay. Sellers are trained to introduce 'add-ons' to the first price that they quote and, if you are careless, you end up paying for 'extras' you had assumed were included. These could include such things as: installation, delivery, packaging, VAT, spares, tools, plugs, different colours, personalised adjustments, insurance, maintenance, warranties.

There are two prices in the selling sequence: the *bait price* to tempt you to buy, and the *over-the-barrel price* (because that's where they've got you) built up from the bait price.

Buyer: I thought you said that the price of this kitchen was £3000?
Seller: That is for the materials only. Your personalised colour scheme costs £500; delivery and installation is £300; then there's VAT at 15 per cent. And I would recommend a two-year service agreement for only £45 a year.

Superdealers find out what the seller intends to give them for their money before, not after, they make a 'buy' decision.

A question such as 'What is included in the price?' forces sellers to reveal the 'add-ons' they otherwise intend to add to the 'bait' price, and also restricts their scope for inventing 'add-ons' if they think you are hooked on buying.

Remember: add-ons are try-ons!

In contrast, Superdealers attack the bait price by turning add-ons into 'take-offs' – there can be 'no deal' unless the quoted price includes everything the seller would normally treat as an add-on.

The inclusion of VAT among the list of potential add-ons might surprise you, but remember, there is no law that says that *you* the buyer must pay the VAT on the sale. The law certainly requires that VAT be paid to the Customs and Excise, and it is certainly normal practice for sellers to add VAT to their selling price and collect it from you. But the requirements of the law are met as long as sellers pay VAT from their sales to the C&E. In other words, sellers can sometimes be persuaded to squeeze their price by agreeing that they, and not you, will pay some or all of the VAT on the sale.

Who asks, gets!

When it comes to the 'buy' decision, you must have the courage to require a concession on the price. If you cannot bring yourself to do this, you reduce your opportunities to pay less for the things you buy.

Courage of this kind does not come easily. If you have never asked for a discount before, it takes some considerable nerve to do so for the first time. But like virginity, once you lose your fear of doing something you have never done before, you will find it much easier to do it again and again, and having gained confidence from doing it once or twice, you might, dare I suggest, enjoy doing it too!

Superdealers always ask for discounts. They don't always get them, but they ask anyway, if only for practice.

Getting over the hurdle of trying for a discount for the first time can be made easier by simply asking:

Do you give discounts for cash?

Naturally, this is not the strongest way you can put it. You are merely seeking information, and the way the question is framed you invite a 'yes' or (more likely) 'no' answer. But the main thing is that you have tried for a discount and broken out of the habit of accepting the tag price without a murmur.

A more positive approach is to ask the same question in a different way:

What discount do you give for cash?

True, they can reply 'None', but the way you have asked the question suggests a greater confidence on your part that you expect a discount from them than merely asking if they give discounts at all – and confidence in the negotiating game is eighty per cent of your leverage.

The stronger approach, and one Superdealers develop with practice, is not to ask a question but to make a statement:

If I am to buy today, I require a 10 per cent discount off the list price.

This tells them the terms of doing business with you. You're not yet quite home and dry, of course, but you have started on the road to a better deal.

If you let a 'no' cower you into submission on subsequent occasions, you should recall the well-known advice to people who fall off bicycles and horses – get up and continue riding, otherwise you'll be too afraid to do so in future. A 'no' should spur you to have another go somewhere else soon – practice at requiring discounts makes it easier to try for one each time.

When Superdealers are determined to get a discount off a tag price, **they are prepared to seek out the person on the selling side who has authority to give a discount**. This could be the manager or, if he or she proves obstinate, it could be the owner of the business.

Obviously, you might need some practice in seeking out discounts before you are confident enough to ask for the manager. But you must start somewhere, so you can try the sales assistant first, even if only by joking about getting one. Many Superdealers began their careers by laughing loudly and saying something such as 'Do I get a discount for using forged money?' Laughter is infectious, and it might be enough to get you through that first barrier we have all faced when we have decided to make a habit of challenging those fixed prices. The assistant might laugh and then call the police, but you have a greater chance of them offering you 5 per cent off.

Common excuses for not giving discounts	*Some responses by determined buyers*
1. 'Why should you get a discount and not the poor pensioner down the road?'	'I am not refusing poor pensioners a discount, I'm asking you for one.' The seller will then try no. 2; respond as below.
2. 'If I give you a discount, I would have to give everybody else one.'	'Would it be acceptable if your spouse refused to kiss you on the same grounds?' (Don't leer!)
3. 'Nobody undersells us as it is, so you can't get it cheaper elsewhere.'	'The never-undersold claim only refers to list prices. Will you beat discount prices?'
4. 'We sell £1 million of these a week.'	'Then a discount on my purchase won't be noticed.'
5. 'Our prices are discounted before they go on display.'	'Give me a discount and you'll achieve a faster turnover.'

Almost all sales assistants will refuse discounts on the usual spurious grounds. They don't always have a lot of discretion, and to be fair, do you think Mr Marks and Mr Spencer got where they did by hiring shop labour reliable enough to quote prices at their own discretion (and most shop staff are not as well trained as those at M & S)?

However, my advice is: persist. Go above the head of the sales assistant to the manager, even if your heart is thumping and you are in great need of a nervous pee. The worst the guy can say is 'no', and for you the experience of asking for a discount once will undoubtedly give you the necessary courage to ask for one again (and again!).

Walking away

From wide experience, I know that, for many supposed sellers, especially those who think they are doing you a favour by serving you at all, the idea of high professional standards in selling is as strange as lust must be for a eunuch. Even a generous comparison of sales behaviour in the United Kingdom with the norm in the United States is so unflattering that it is best left unmade. Sales staff talking to each other while serving customers is not just rude, it's also bad for business; waiters who avoid eye contact with a diner desperate to attract their attention reduce their chances of a tip . . . and their customer's patience to breaking point.

The fact remains, however, that the seller is in business to sell goods, not treat them as museum pieces, and enquiries about special deals ('How much off for the model in the window?') should appeal to the successful seller's most basic belief: *a sale trumps a 'no-sale'*. Unfortunately, the behaviour of many sellers suggests they believe that a 'no-sale' is not a disaster: *if you don't buy, they believe somebody else will.*

I was told, while drafting this chapter, that the gross weekly sales of a store I was trying to do business with were £1.5 million. The seller told me this, not because he thought I was interested in his company's financial performance, but in order to demonstrate how unimportant was my custom and my insistence that I wouldn't buy the £15 clock-radio unless he gave me a free plug with it. (I stood my ground, of course, and when he conceded the free plug, I bought the radio!)

Superdealers look for, and ask for, special deals.

A special deal is one that is appropriate for you and the seller in the circumstances. You are not asking for a better deal for everybody else, nor are you setting a precedent. Your confident suggestion is solely concerned with securing a better deal for you. It could be based on almost anything that is relevant to the main transaction and realistic enough to prompt the seller into agreeing:

Give me a new set of tyres and I'll take the van.

If you give me a special price, I'll place my order right now.

I'll take last year's model if you take 15 per cent off.

Give me a double room, don't charge for the kids, and we'll stay a week.

If you give me a year's free maintenance, I'll buy the deluxe model.

Tell you what: use the higher grade stone at the normal price, and you can place a sign board with your company name on it outside my house for three months.

How much off the price if I take delivery of a year's supply now?

If you use your imagination when discussing the deal, you can find all kinds of 'specials' to go for.

Remember, your chances of getting a better deal are improved if the seller appreciates the true role of sales in their working life. This is, to put it bluntly, to so arrange a transaction that they get your money out of your purse or pocket and into their till. It is remarkable how often sellers forget this (which is why sales training is a lucrative business), and sometimes you have to find ways of reminding them of their true role, subtly if you can, unambiguously if you must.

One way to cultivate your skill is to wrap your request for a special deal in the form of a commitment from you that, if he or she concedes something, you are prepared to help them realise their true goal (to move cash from you to them). Otherwise you won't.

Now, not all sellers (by a large margin) are willing to do a deal, even if it means they lose a sale. Their employers have forgotten what they are in business for, or if they remember, they have become confused.

In general, when this happens you must, except in the most pressing of circumstances (e.g. the last plane from Beirut), *be prepared to walk away from the seller and take your business elsewhere.* It is sometimes inconvenient to do so, but you will never be free of the tyranny of fixed prices, nor the impossibility of living within your current income, unless you are prepared to stand up for a better deal. If you have a choice and the guy says 'no' and means it even though your request was quite modest, you must not give them your business.

Should you let the matter drop there and go off in search of a more sensible seller? Is walking away enough? I do not think so.

You will experience stress from a deadlocked deal and it is good therapy to get it off your chest. Wandering the town rehearsing all the things you should have said and felt like saying will do you less good than:

• telling the seller directly why you are not doing business with them.

• writing to the chief executive about it (but briefly please;

'busy executives' read no more than four paragraphs from customers, not their entire life stories).

Some people believe that you should not help a bad business to survive by pointing out to them any defects in their performance. I do not subscribe to this view. Company executives love to demonstrate their authority to take 'executive action' and your letter might encourage them to do so. When I bought my word processor I had a lot of trouble convincing the printer-ribbon, paper and daisy wheel supplier that I ought not to be treated the same way as a large company in terms of minimum ordering quantities but I should be in respect of the discounts they were offering. My machine is solely used for book and letter writing and does not go through the same quantities of supplies as one in a busy commercial office.

Unable to get through the local red tape and the seller's lack of discretion in price, I wrote to the managing director and asked if he would tell his people to let me buy smaller quantities of supplies at quantity discount prices. Otherwise I would cease to buy the more expensive proprietary brand supplies and switch to competing brands. He wrote back declining the full discount but authorising the supply of smaller quantities. He also sent a *free* month's supply of printer ribbons – at my rate of usage they lasted three months! – as a friendly gesture.

You should regard your activities in this respect – refusing a deal, walking away and letting them know why – as part of the campaign you are undertaking on behalf of (primarily) yourself, and also, in a sense, on behalf of everybody else.

Sellers who are about to say 'no' can be educated into the realisation that saying 'no' to a Superdealer is no way to get a Superdealer to say 'yes'. It's not just a 'no-sale' – of which there are many examples in any seller's day – when they refuse to bargain with you; it's a 'lost' sale – which, given the behaviour of 97 per cent of the buying public, is a rare event in their selling careers. It may be that they don't yet know the difference between a no-sale (didn't want to buy the goods) and a lost sale (couldn't come to an agreement on the bargain), but telling them – and their head office – helps to educate them. They know now that they could have done business with you if only they had bargained.

If, however, you crumble and buy at the first or even the final 'no' you hear from a seller in the great theatre of negotiation, you will forever be a victim of your own stage fright. What's more, they won't even notice your discomfort, and that's got to be bad for you, and for them.

Your checklist

A Superdeal strategy is basically quite simple – so simple that it's amazing that so many people are unaware of the power they could have, and the income they would save to spend on other things, if only they practised it.

If you want to become a Superdealer:

- *Decide* why you want to buy the goods in the first place.
- *Choose* factual reasons for your purchase rather than emotional ones.
- *Survey* what is on offer in whatever time is available.
- *Never praise* a seller's product.
- *Disclose* how the product only partially meets your needs.
- *Identify* what is included and what excluded in the seller's first price.
- Always *require* a discount or some other concession.
- *Seek out* who has authority to give discounts.
- *Look for and suggest* special deals.
- *Do without* the product, even if inconvenienced, if the seller says 'no' to your reasonable offers.

2

Beat 'em!

Most households accumulate furniture, carpets, curtains, kitchen equipment, cleaning tools, general linen goods and so on. Mostly, you must spend money to acquire these items, and in doing so you come up against professional sales staff. Their advantage over the average buyer is that they practise their selling skills every day, but Superdealers have the edge because most sellers will not be expecting to deal with someone who knows what they are about.

The mark-up on, for example, furniture in High Street retail shops is in excess of 40 per cent, leaving considerable scope for a negotiation on the price (for proof, check 'sale' and discount warehouse prices). Superdealers require 10 per cent off as a matter of course:

If you give me a 10 per cent discount, I'll buy it.

or:

If you take £15 off, I'll buy it.

They might say 'yes', or suggest a lower discount (leaving you ahead compared to those who don't bother to ask), or say 'no', and give you one spurious reason or another to justify their refusal. All is not lost, however, for against every move there is always a counter (the final one is to take your business elsewhere).

The seller may be unwilling to give you a price discount on the piece of furniture that you have been examining because they do not sell from the display stock in the shop. Why should this matter? The traditional system for selling furniture in the UK works like this: the seller displays examples of a manufacturer's products, takes orders from customers and passes the orders on to the manufacturer. On receipt of orders, the manufacturer produces the furniture and eventually supplies the retailers and, through them, the customers. The manufacturer's profit is built into the wholesale price, which is marked-up in the shop by 40 per cent or more. The difference between the retail price quoted to you and the wholesale price covers selling costs, taxes and rates, and leaves a residual as profit. Discounts, we are told, squeeze the retail shop's profits.

The truth is different: while a discount on a particular item does reduce their *rate* of profit, because it encourages a sale it leads to faster turnover and, therefore, higher total profits.

Manufacturing to order builds delays into the system, though it reduces costs and risks to the manufacturer. It also means, of course, that you have to wait for the goods that you buy. When do you pay for the furniture that you order? When the furniture is delivered to the shop, or when it is ordered?

Businesses that require you to pay when the goods are de-livered expose themselves to the risk that you will change your mind before they deliver, leaving them with the expense of producing the (now unwanted) goods. 'Modern' stores get the customer to finance, or part finance, the transaction.

For instance, if the factory is paid in advance, it is able to use your money to fund its business by avoiding laying out its own (or its bank's) money to manufacture your new furniture. That has to be a wheeze of a scheme! Also, when you have to pay in advance, the retail shop is assured of its profit from your order. Psychologically, as they hold your money as an advance pay-ment, they hold most of the aces.

The holder of your money, be it the shop or the supplier, uses your money in the meantime. In fact, advance payment schemes are so profitable a means of funding a business that some manu-facturers sell their wares through their own retail shops and use their customers' advance payments for their entire working capital.

Advance payment discounts

Getting you to pay in advance is by far the most profitable system for sellers of furniture, central heating, double glazing, building extensions, yachts and holidays, but you still have scope for an assault on the price. And assault it you must, because if you don't, the final price will be higher than the one you think you are paying.

Sellers (though, alas, not the VAT man) know that nothing is sold until it's paid for, and anything can happen, and often does, in between you drooling over the brochure in the shop and the goods arriving at your house. For example, suppose the seller quotes 'ten-to-twelve-week delivery' for a 'lovely' Chesterfield-style sofa. It is more likely that you will see the sofa after the twelfth week than by the tenth, as delivery promises are totally unreliable and only believed by the gullible. Thus, whenever a seller requires payment in advance, the inevitable delivery delay enables you to press for an *advance payment discount*.

Briefly, tell them that, if they want the use of your money for three months, you require a discount off the price for the cost to you of doing without the use of your money. How do you make the case for a discount? First, convince yourself that you have a case, and second, talk figures to them in a way that shows that you know what you are talking about.

Don't underestimate the importance of having an inner conviction that you have a very strong case – any doubts that you may have will creep into your voice and body posture like alcohol. And what sellers can see, or sense, they play to. Consider the situation: by giving the shop your money for twelve weeks, you are giving up the opportunity to earn interest on your money in a savings account, i.e. you are foregoing an opportunity to lend money to a bank or building society at a profit to yourself. By using your money for twelve weeks for nothing, the shop is getting a free loan from you instead of a pricey one from a bank. Now, the two things that you know for certain are:

1. Banks do not borrow your money for nothing, so why should the shop do so?
2. Banks do not lend money to anybody for nothing, so why should you do so?

How much should you be paid for the use of your money? This depends on your negotiation with the shop, but one thing is sure: if you don't attempt to get them to pay for the use of your money, they certainly won't offer to compensate you for borrowing it for nothing.

There are two considerations here: the amount you could earn by placing your money in a savings account, and the amount a bank would charge the shop for borrowing the money you pay them in advance. These amounts give the range within which your required discount is negotiated.

Suppose you want to buy a sofa priced £500 and the shop quotes you a ten-to-twelve-week delivery delay and requires that you pay the full amount in advance. How do you set about building your case?

If banks are offering 8 per cent on deposit accounts, the way to figure out the cost of your £500 loan to the shop is:

For every £100 on deposit, the bank will give me £8 a year in interest, and as I have £500 available for deposit in the bank, the total interest I could earn is $5 \times £8 = £40$. The shop proposes to hold my £500 for 12 weeks, about a quarter of a year, which means that it costs me ¼ of £40 or £10 (approximately) in lost interest on my savings.

On this basis, the sofa should be priced at about £490, consisting of the £490 cash you pay in advance plus the £10 that the shop earns from the use of your money. Without a price discount, you would actually pay £510 for a £500 sofa (your £500 cash plus £10 in lost interest that you donate to the shop). This isn't very smart, is it? What would you say if they said that the sofa was priced £500 but, in an arbitrary binge of wilful price-hiking, they were charging £510 for it? Why, therefore, let a hidden price-hike pass without a struggle?

Now calculate what your free loan is worth to the shop:

For every £100 borrowed by the shop from a bank, it will be charged about £16 a year interest. As they are borrowing £500 from me, the total annual cost to the shop would be $5 \times £16 = £80$ if they went to a bank. The shop proposes to hold my money for 12 weeks, which means they save themselves ¼ of £80 or £20 (approximately) in bank interest charges from my free loan.

Here the hidden price rise is even clearer. They charge you £500 for a sofa and use your money to avoid bank charges of £20, which means that selling sofas to people who pay in advance reduces the shop's borrowings by £20 a time at absolutely no cost to themselves.

With proper control of the financing of the shop's operations, it makes profits from those of its customers (the majority) who agree to pay in advance for their goods, and, perversely, it also has no incentive to push the factory to deliver on time. Only customer goodwill – a notoriously elusive virtue – compels the shop to promote its customers' interests.

When many tens (possibly hundreds) of thousands of pounds are held as advance payments, a retail chain can make good profits by being better at selling sofas than at delivering them, and those of you who have become demented with rage at the failure of deliveries from furniture stores can now see why the stores appear to be so 'helpless' in chasing suppliers. All delays in the shop having to pay the factory for orders it placed three months before are a profitable sideline for the retailer.

A well-known wine company made more money for years by banking, for a month or more, the cash flow from its branches than it did from the profit on the wine it sold. This was especially true once it reached so high a volume of business that it could negotiate forty-five days' credit on the wine it bought from its suppliers in France.

In summary, the financing of the sofa costs you £10 and saves them £20. There is the basis of a negotiation here.

The minimum advance payment discount you go for is, of course, £10 (the amount that the transaction costs you) and the maximum you can hope to get is £20 (what the transaction saves the shop). Where you open is up to you, taking into consideration how desperate you think they are to sell the sofa and how keen you are to buy it. Superdealers, of course, are never too enthusiastic about a product they wish to buy – it only encourages sellers to say 'no' to discounts.

Price discounts

Suppose, however, you are dealing with a retail shop that takes orders for tables and requires payment only when the goods are delivered? Should you press for a discount *when you order?*

No.

The balance of power is not in your favour at that moment because the seller can defend his prices up to the moment that he instructs the manufacturer to undertake the costs of producing your table. Sellers always say 'no' to a discount for a hypothetical sale.

True, in saying 'no' he might lose a sale, but experience teaches sellers that most customers don't ask for discounts, and most of those that do take 'no' for an answer; thus, the risk of losing the sale is small. However, if he does lose the sale as a result of saying 'no', he also avoids a financial obligation to the manufacturer, who requires to be paid on delivery of the table to the shop.

Many more people visit a shop and examine its wares than place orders. Losing your specific order may not be such a big deal for a shop if they lose it during the preliminary stages of the sale. Your negotiating leverage at the beginning of a sale is lost in the crowd of people who look but don't buy – nothing is sold until it's paid for. You only become important to the seller after he has undertaken some obligation to the manufacturer, or has invested considerable time in showing you his wares.

The situation changes, however, when you return to pay for the table. Now you can go for a price discount because you have the power at that moment.

Since I ordered the table we have acquired a new sideboard and there is less room for it, but if you take 10 per cent off for cash, I'll still take it.

I see the list price for this table is £240. Make that £220 and you've got a cash sale.

They have a table, which they have paid, or are about to pay, their supplier for manufacturing, and they also have a potential customer for the table in the shop. When, in these different circumstances, they say 'no' to a request for a modest discount, they have no hold on you for the amount that they owe (or have paid) the manufacturer, and if they are obstinate, they can be left with an unsold table. They know this. True, you can end up without a table, but you have the money and, having done without a table while the one you ordered was being manufactured, you can hardly be totally desperate.

You can strengthen your negotiating position with the shop if you delay responding to their notice that your table is ready for collection. Wait a week at least, longer if possible. Rushing in the very morning they tell you the table has arrived, flushed with enthusiasm to see 'your' table, hardly helps you put pressure on them for a price discount!

When, however, they say 'yes' to your request for a modest discount, they know that the table is sold and that they can pay what they owe the manufacturer and take their gross profit, probably still over 40 per cent after your modest discount.

If they demur, or threaten retaliation (hints of a visit to Messrs Waist, Phee & Sue) make it easier for them to see the sense of giving you a modest discount by hinting at a spoilt relationship for refusing you less than what they offer everybody each year during their winter sales.

'I KNOW YOU GOT A TWO PERCENT DISCOUNT BUT ISN'T THREE YEARS RATHER LONG TO WAIT FOR DELIVERY?'

Immediate delivery discounts

You can still go for a price discount even when the seller requires customers to pay a deposit on the furniture they order before it is manufactured. Here, the balance of power, nominally, is in favour of the seller, because he holds some of the cash. The deposit is a hostage against a deadlock over the price. But there is a weakness in this system and you might be able to exploit it if the opportunity arises.

The deposit system works in such a way that if, say, when the table arrives in the shop you decide not to buy it (i.e. pay the balance you owe the shop) you forfeit your deposit. The threat of this happening is what motivates you to complete the transaction. But what does the seller do with the tables or whatever that are not bought, despite customers forfeiting their deposits? He may be lucky and find another customer who wants to order exactly the same table as the one left on his hands, in which case he switches names on the tickets and drops a note to the second customer that 'his' table awaits him. On the other hand, providence is not always kind to sellers left with unsold stock, and they have to work a little harder at moving their unsold goods. The shop then tries to sell off the table as something available for immediate delivery to any customer who is willing to accept it.

If you are the kind of customer who is shocked into bliss by the discovery that the shop actually has something in stock that you can take away with you that very day, instead of the usual three-month wait, in your euphoria you could be missing a Superdeal.

In a large retail operation, there is always somebody who has failed to complete a purchase even at risk of losing their deposit. Remember, in furniture buying (and in booking package holidays, for example) people change their minds, move to another district, run away from their spouse or even die in the interim. These not-uncommon events undo deals made perhaps several months earlier, and the cash deposit is no barrier to a cop-out – nobody stays in a bad marriage, or ignores the Lord's final call, just for a £50 deposit on a table!

When you hear that you can get immediate delivery of a table on display, though normally it takes weeks to get them delivered, *you know that some other customer ordered the table but did not complete the sale.* You also know that the shop has already pocketed a part-payment for the table by the customer, and that it must sell the table, somewhat quickly, to recover the balance of the cash it owes, or has already paid, to the manufacturer.

The minimum price it can accept, when added to the deposit, only has to be enough to pay the manufacturer and cover its selling costs, which together are considerably less than the table's list price.

This is your opportunity to go for a discount and, in the circumstances, it is unlikely that the seller will say 'no', if only to clear his books. At a minimum, as long as the discount you want is smaller than the deposit the other customer paid (which can be calculated by asking what is the normal deposit paid on orders), the seller must say 'yes' if he gets enough cash to cover his obligations. You might even be offered a discount without asking for one (though *never* rely on this happening) if you were to take the table off his hands quickly. *This should make you ask for a little more*, as the discount they first think of is always smaller than the one they are prepared to settle for!

See how they react to an offer to pay with a credit card for the special offer (credit card companies charge a 2 to 5 per cent commission). If they say 'yes', they have more discount in reserve (up the ante by 3 per cent immediately). If they say 'no', you know they are close to their limit – or, perhaps, they're bluffing?

It may be worth the seller's while to allow a larger discount than the deposit the other customer paid. For instance, once finance charges begin (adding to his bank borrowings) on the money he has used to pay the manufacturer, there is mounting pressure on the seller to settle for something to stem further losses. Super-dealers call this the *haemorrhage close*: 'I'll stop you bleeding to death, but it'll cost you a modest discount.'

Do not be timid in the amount of discount you go for unless, for instance, you are trying out this move for the first time and want to walk before you run. 'Walking' might mean a try for a £10 (or even £1) discount, and if you are wondering whether this is worth fussing about, it is! If you see a £10 note in the street, do you step over it and leave it for somebody else? It's not hard work to get a discount – a few minutes' determined conversation can get one, without a drop of sweat in sight. More importantly, while the sums involved in a discount might appear small, the very same methods can be used to negotiate big-value discounts when the stakes are higher (houses, cars, divorce settlements and so on). But if, in a misguided belief that it is 'beneath you' to haggle, you refrain from acquiring practice in negotiating for the smaller stakes, your lack of practice when it comes to negotiating for anything that matters will surely show.

Superdealers take the view that trying for a discount of £10, or even £1, does matter, particularly as, in the case of the advance payment discount, the same method can be applied to many more transactions than just the purchase of furniture. Think, for example, of the advance payments sellers require for house decoration, travel and holidays, and almost anything else that you have to pay for and then wait for delivery.

Getting a grip on these very real and, in the aggregate, very large costs helps to reduce expenditure on many items, releasing the cash saved for other things. By saving money on basic expenditures, Superdealing makes your income go further.

Discount warehouses

Discount furniture warehouses have become popular in the last few years. These operate away from the High Street with its escalating rates and expensive shopfittings. A large run-down warehouse in a run-down district is sufficient for selling furniture at what appear to be lower prices than those found more centrally. What's more, discount stores sell direct from stock with no delivery delays (though they try to get you to pay for delivery to your house). However, don't let the store kid you that they are already selling their stock at rock-bottom prices. Their margins may be slightly lower than High Street stores' but so are their selling costs.

You can see the extent of the mark-up in these so-called 'low-priced' discount stores when you look at their 'sale' prices. These reductions can vary between 15 and 35 per cent on their 'normal' discount prices for the duration of the 'sale'!

Discount stores are interested in volume business, and need to be as they carry a large stock that they must turn over in six weeks or so if they are to stay in business. Tables and chairs that are not moving represent dead capital to them and a charge on their profitability. Their aim is to turn over their capital as quickly as they can, if not sooner. Because they are prepared to sell you single items of furniture, *but prefer to sell you several items*, you have a chance to negotiate.

Many people faced with discounted prices combine their purchases, using the money they save on one purchase as a means to make another purchase. Go for a *combined purchase discount* off the total purchase – a set of chairs *and* a table, or even two disparate items such as a bed and a set of kitchen stools.

You waste your negotiating power if you wander round the store listing all the items you want to purchase and then total the cost at the counter. You are forgetting the store's main interest: moving stock as fast as they can.

Sales assistants at a crowded counter are not the best people from whom to get a combined purchase discount (it's difficult enough to get their attention). You need them to come out from behind the counter. However, the stores know that they are in a more defensible position price-wise if their staff stay behind the counter solely to check off your requirements, total the bill and take your money. Discount stores want the price to do the selling, not their staff.

How do you get them out from behind the counter? By having a query ready that requires them to accompany you to the displays. Suppose you are interested in a table and chairs. Start with the price for a single chair and then move to a discount for four chairs: 'With 10 per cent off, I'll think about taking four chairs – you do have four in stock?' If he says 'no' to your offer and means it, you are talking to the wrong person. Ask to see the manager. The manager, scenting a large order, might offer you a small discount – and to Superdealers *all* discounts are a victory, though bigger discounts are bigger victories!

It may be necessary to enlarge the scope of your purchase at this point: you're not just a potential buyer of the chairs; you might buy a table as well! *It is most unlikely that he will refuse to move on his price when he is sure that you are serious about a purchase if you get something off the price.* He is also unlikely to refuse to discount because he is against price-shaving in principle (perish the thought!), though he may try to snow you with statements about the price on the tags 'already being heavily discounted, that's why we're called a discount store' (quoted to me recently by a manager in his ultimately futile refusal of a discount on a spin dryer).

He may be under hidden (from you) pressures emanating from the accountants at head office to move his stock. He is really under pressure when there is a 'sale' going on. That's what a sale is for: to release the capital tied up in 'dead' stock. The absence of 'sale' signs, however, does not mean that the store manager is not under severe pressure. Unless you have been at the receiving end of an accountant showering you with financial ratios, you may mistakenly believe that only your boss has a PhD in nagging!

At any one time, every store (discount or otherwise) has some items that are moving too slowly for the accountant's stress levels, and the store will sell them at a discount (even on top of the already announced discount) to move them faster. If this ploy does not work fast enough (and accountants expect everything to happen yesterday), the manager knows he can help his monthly sales quotas by moving his faster-selling items a little quicker. Hence, he is in the market to sell even a quick selling item at a bigger discount than is implied on the price tag. So require one, and don't take 'no' for an answer until he throws you out of the door! Your request for a (modest) combined purchase discount for goods that are moving slowly, and one for those that are moving quickly, meets the main needs of the seller: shifting goods and raising turnover to get the bloody accountants off his back.

You can buy 'sale' goods from a discount warehouse at an additional discount by noting if the store displays credit card signs. This tells you that if you pay cash or by cheque, it should be willing to cut at least 3 per cent off its 'sale' price to take into account the commission it won't have to pay the credit card company for operating its facilities.

Not only does the fact that a store accepts credit cards provide a strong counter to the refrain that 'all prices are already discounted to their limits', credit cards also prove the case for the combined purchase discount. The reason why discount stores are prepared to pay the credit card company at least 3 per cent of the amount spent by card holders is precisely because credit cards motivate customers to spend more than cash customers. What the store loses in the 3 per cent commission, it more than makes up for in higher turnover from credit card customers.

You can see this yourself by considering which is better for the store manager: a cash sale of £50 for a small table or a credit sale of £150 for a small table, a bookcase and a kitchen chair? The cash sale of £50 gives him (say) £15 towards profit, while the credit sale costs him £4.50 in commission but increases the sale's contribution to profit to, say, £45.

By offering him a cash purchase and *not using your credit card*, you aim for a minimum of a 3 per cent discount, leaving the seller no worse off than if you used your credit card. What possible reason would he have for saying 'no'? Hence, try for 5 per cent. You can be sure that the manager will think about the extra £30 contribution to his profit from selling you the bookcase and the kitchen chair, and that he knows he might even blow the deal if he provokes you into not buying the small table because he tells you he prefers to give the credit card company the £4.50 rather than discounting it back to you.

How to get more by adding on

Another buying technique used by Superdealers is the *add-on*. The add-on can be used:

- in combination with a try for a discount.
- by itself if the store will not budge on price.
- if you have insufficient time to try for a discount.

With the add-on, you search for something (it does not have to be of very high value) that has an obvious relationship to the higher-valued basic item you are purchasing. A concession from the store on the add-on is your condition for buying at all.

Some examples of add-ons are suggested below (but note that the add-on also works in garages, hotels, restaurants, general stores, in fact almost anywhere that suppliers have more than one product in their range):

If you throw in the set of pillows, I'll buy the bed.

If you give me 50 per cent off the curtain rails, I'll buy four sets of curtains.

Fit a plug to the lamp and give me some bulbs and we have a deal.

My husband likes the candlesticks on the table, so include them in the deal and we'll take it.

I shall return to the add-on several times as we go on. *An ability to 'add-on' is one of the surest signs that you have grasped the Superdeal message.* Using your imagination creatively and practising the add-on everywhere you can does more for your negotiating performance than almost any other technique.

Free delivery

Stores vary in practice regarding who pays for delivery. Some include delivery in the price; others make a separate charge for it. Delivery certainly costs somebody something – the driver's wages, the running cost of the vehicle and the accounting charge for depreciation – and what appears to be 'free' is paid for in the price of the goods.

First, find out what is included in any price they want to charge for their goods ('what do I get for my money?'). A charge for delivery is nothing more than one of *their* add-ons (and you know why they add-on!), so change it into a demand for a 'take-off' by requiring free delivery if you are to buy the things that they want to sell to you.

Some stores have separated out the delivery function from their own operation by contracting it to independent operators. This has the advantage for them of putting the cost of transport directly on to you and preventing you from pushing them for an additional concession.

Many of these independent operators consist of the owner or, indeed, hirer of a light van and a mate working for wages. You seldom see the van owner until the items are delivered to your house. All you hear from the shop is that the agreed price for the furniture (or whatever) only gives you ownership; it's up to you to remove the goods from the shop. If you need help to remove the goods, they can put you on to a delivery service that will charge you, say, £5, but the removal people are not part of the shop's operation and any problems you have over the delivery are between you and the transport company. Your alternative is to remove the goods yourself.

Can this situation be overcome?

Perhaps it can, for although delivery is arranged through an independent operator, there is no reason why you have to pay for delivery of the goods the shop wants you to buy. Whether they pay the charge depends on how keen they are to sell their goods – if the sale is going to turn into a 'no-sale' on the delivery charge, they might be persuaded to pick up the tab themselves. It's up to you to suggest this, for if you don't, nobody is going to offer it to you.

What if delivery is 'free', can you still go for a discount?

Sure you can, for if delivery is 'free', the cost of delivery is included in the price of the goods (otherwise delivery costs would come out of the seller's profits) and, therefore, you can try for a discount for removing the items yourself.

Naturally, a discount for using your own rather than the store's delivery service is more credible if the items are really bulky – such as a large carpet or a lot of heavy furniture. A couple of curtain rails are hardly going to be a credible lever while pursuing the 'free' delivery discount. Similarly, a discount for self-delivery is more likely to be credible if the order is for a very large value item (whether it is bulky or not is irrelevant), particularly something from stock that the store wants to get rid of. They might be persuaded to discount the price for self-delivery in order to complete a sought-after sale.

Your options

Superdealers have options when negotiating for basic needs, and these give them bargaining leverage, even in those product lines that are believed to be basic to minimal comforts.

Your first option always is to *postpone a purchase decision*. This might be inconvenient for you but it will also be worrying for the seller. Potential buyers who are not sold the first time are seldom sold a second time.

But just how inconvenient is it for you to postpone purchasing, say, a bed? If the alternative is sleeping on the floorboards, you might think you have no choice but to accept the overpriced bed the seller is shoving your way. Instead, you should give yourself a choice! Buy a second-hand mattress while you continue the hunt for a sensible seller of beds. The alternative to buying a new bed to replace an old one is to continue with your current sleeping arrangements. Deciding to buy a new bed and insisting on buying one that very day, no matter what it costs, is not too sensible a way of acquiring negotiating leverage.

It's always better to give the impression to the seller that you *might* buy a bed (or, for that matter, anything else) rather than that you *must* buy one.

We were thinking of replacing our bed, *which is perfectly good for a few more years*, but if you have something that we like, we might consider doing business with you.

is far more effective than:

If I don't buy a new bed today to replace the one that collapses every time one of us turns over, my wife is going to leave me tonight.

Ask yourself: which of the above makes the seller keener to make concessions to get a sale?

If you don't like what the seller has to offer, you can *take your business elsewhere* (probably the most under-used option of all!). How many furniture shops are there in your town? Provide yourself with options by finding out what is on offer around town and let the seller know that you are not just aware of the options but that you are willing to go to his rivals and buy their carpets.

Sellers are aware that searching for a suitable purchase costs buyers a great deal of time and trouble, and they know that, in the main, they can rely on most buyers not to go elsewhere if they are offered more or less what they want (which often means selling you something just outside your price range). Half-hearted attempts to challenge a price can be batted off by the seller if the alternative for the buyer is to start the entire process over again somewhere else.

Superdealers never give the impression of being about to give up the search for a better deal elsewhere. They cut out advertisements from the local paper of the rival companies in their district. They display these in the showroom while comparing what is being offered by the seller as he makes his pitch. They do not react to disparaging remarks that are made by the seller about his rivals. They look at their watches occasionally to put some pressure on the seller and hint that they are about to go across town and take the deal they have been offered.

It is the perceptions of the seller about your intentions that count, not whether this or that aspect of your behaviour is true or false. You may be worn down with your search, but it should never show. There are no remarks like: 'Thank God, you've got a carpet in that colour. I've looked everywhere for one until I'm sick of looking.' What does that tell the seller? Well, it hardly motivates him to make a concession to get the sale!

Another option you have is to *purchase a second-hand item rather than a new one.*

Access to the wider market for second-hand goods is your greatest option of all. Exercise it when you want to, and bear this option in mind when pressed towards a 'buy' decision for a basic need by a seller who is sticking to his price. You will save precious cash from the purchase of basic needs, which can be used for the purchase of less pressing but more enjoyable things.

3
Turning tables

As our society has got richer, we have substituted machinery for man (or, in this case, woman) power. More women than ever before have, or seek, paid work, which means they have a desire to cut the burden in energy and time of doing unpaid housework. The result: a mass industry of products that are 'essential' in every household. Lack of these products can make any person without them a slave to domestic drudgery.

The extent to which households have acquired these types of goods varies across income groups, though just about all have acquired some of them. Cookers, fridges and hoovers probably lead the field, followed by washing machines, spin dryers, freezers, dishwashers and, latterly, microwave ovens. You are likely to be in the market for one or other of these goods at least once a year, either to replace an old one or to acquire a new piece of kit for the comfort and ease of the family. Given their expense, they are an obvious target for a Superdealer.

The buying problems are familiar. You have to select something from an often bewildering range of brands on offer, for which you want to pay as little as you can for the one you think best suits your circumstances, and you don't want to buy a 'lemon'. In the store, you are assaulted on all fronts by a marketing plan that its creators spent thousands to put together – they recoup the costs from the customers – designed to get you into an emotional, not a rational, mood for buying. Sid Slick, and his associates, have rehearsed their acts for long enough. They have heard every objection to a 'buy' decision from every kind of customer. And they are in practice.

You're on your own, and it's all uphill from the moment you walk into the store. You had better be ready for them with a Superdeal. Otherwise, they'll blow a hole in your finances.

How to panic a seller into conceding

Spell out your reasons for buying anything before you start looking for a deal. Test how badly you really want it, and to what lengths, in a cash sense, you'll go to get it.

Consider also the possibilities of acquiring what you want from the second-hand market. For example, if you are considering a microwave, check their used prices in the small ads. If the price difference is favourable, is it worth a look to see what state the oven is in, and to check why they are selling it? Look in the small ads, too, to see which brands of washing machine feature most. Is it a good or a bad sign that one or two brands feature regularly? Does this compromise their image of reliability, or does it indicate market leadership by an efficient brand?

In the store, Sid Slick and his pals search for your 'buy button', which tells him which sales line to use to meet your declared or suspected needs. He listens for 'buy' signals emanating from you or whomsoever you're with ('It would fit into the space beside the fridge'; 'I like the pale green finish'; 'Mary has a chip fryer just like that'; 'We've looked at the rest and this one suits us', etc.). Slick will not be expecting you to have a Superdeal strategy, and he will unwittingly respond positively to your needs – a better deal for you – like the proverbial Pavlovian dog.

Superdealers remember (and practise):

The longer you can prevent disclosure of your buying intentions (no 'ooing' and 'aahing' please; no direct statement that you will buy; no disclosure of pressing needs or felt desires) *the more concessions* (special offers, interest-free loans, free supplies of accessory products, longer warranties, better parts and labour guarantees, etc.) *the seller will offer before you commit yourself.*

Once you say 'I'll buy it', or emit a definite buying signal such as how you warm to the product and how you talk to each other about it, Slick switches off all thought of concessions. When you indicate your decision to buy too soon:

Seller: Can I help you?
Buyer: I've come to buy the new Washington multibake cooker adver-
          tised on TV. Do you sell them?

you'll be stung for the list price, plus any add-ons he can get. Slick makes a small fortune from his add-ons – 'containers', special fluids, powders, filters, spare blades, plugs and stands – and all at list prices. Your best bet, therefore, is to shut up and let him throw them at you in an effort to get you to say 'yes'.

Open the discussions with:

Seller: Can I help you?
Buyer: Maybe. We're thinking of replacing our cooker so we'll browse
          round the ones you have here.

Slick will hover close by, ready at the raising of an eyebrow to leap in and try to sell you the cooker of *his* choice at list price.

While you remain unimpressed and uncommitted, he will shower you with offers ('special discount if you order today', 'free gift of a clock-radio with the deluxe model', etc.). If he believes you are not going to buy, panic sets in. He is below quota this week, and that is like having galloping halitosis as far as Slick's relations with Tricky Dicky, his sales manager, are concerned.

If, in response to his concessions, you let him off the hook and hint at a sale, Slick relaxes, and stops conceding anything. Indeed, he tries to pull a few back with some add-ons:

- 'That's £500 less the special discount of £65, *plus delivery and installation*, making it £490.'
- 'The free installation only covers the first three feet of gas pipe; *after that*, I'm afraid, *there is a labour charge.*'
- 'The clock-radio only comes with the deluxe model; with this one, *you only get an alarm clock.*'

As soon as you sign the order, Slick mentally begins to spend the bonus your decision gets him, which is how Tricky Dicky likes his sellers to behave. The hungrier they are, and the faster they spend their money, preferably while in abject debt, the better they are at reaching their sales targets – 'It's harder on the foot to kick fat asses than scraggy ones' is how Tricky puts it.

Superdealers raise Slick's state of panic and, therefore, the rate of his concessions by:

- asking him: 'Is this your *entire* range?'
- prominently displaying a sheet of paper with the names and addresses of all dealers in cookers in your town, with prices and deals pencilled in the margin. (Slick learned how to read upside down before he needed to shave.)

Sid Slick is not used to people who seem to know something about the market. Most people wander in, listen to his patter, fall in love with the cooker of his choice and pay the list price. Your behaviour, being different, and his panic, being unusual, encourages him to make concessions.

If he sees a rival's leaflet for a cooker that he sells with a price written on it that is less than his, he will either go for a matching price, or let you 'add on' extras (delivery, installation, set of pots, etc.). Slick is like a junkie needing a fix; he must get a sale if he possibly can; otherwise, he's on Tricky Dicky's Monday morning interview list, again.

In Sid Slick's opinion, it's never a moment too soon for you to send a 'buy' signal, for he must make up the lower profits he has conceded on your deal with list price profits from other buyers he's going to meet that day.

Fortunately for Superdealers, not all sellers, nor even a majority, are as good as Slick and they often miss a 'buy' signal. Many sellers, not all of them beginners, rabbit on with their pat selling sequences, oblivious to the danger of making the sale unprofitable for themselves or, in extreme cases of tedium-induced 'selling', of losing the sale they actually made. Someday, Slick will become a sales manager, like Tricky Dicky, and he will give average and worse sellers a hard time. In the meantime, you can give him a hard time and make him work really hard at selling whatever you choose to buy and at a lower price than the one he first thought of.

How sellers get you to say 'yes'

If you think Sid Slick is easy meat, think again. He is no pushover; forget this and you'll visit the cleaners.

Let's look at some of the techniques Slick uses to get you to say 'yes'. In sales training, these are called 'closes'. A *close* moves the buyer to a 'buy' decision. There are literally thousands of closes, perhaps as many as there are buyers. New closes are invented every day to press somebody's 'buy button'.

It is not that buyers don't want to buy whatever they end up with. After all, it is essential that you have some intention, no matter how vague, to buy before Slick gets going; otherwise he's likely to be wasting his time. True, there are legendary stories about some of Slick's predecessors (and he tells new staff these stories, only he's now in the leading role – he heard them first from Tricky Dicky) who sold things to people who had absolutely no intention of buying at all. Indeed, in the seller's equivalent of Grimms' Fairy Tales, some of these buyers were totally hostile to the product – before, that is, Slick got to work to find, or create, a 'buy button'.

Many people enter stores to view; fewer enter to buy. But the majority of viewers are prospective buyers and yet many leave without buying for any of a dozen reasons:

Why the customer didn't buy	Seller's counter
Too high a price.	Use the 'cheap or low-cost' close.
Shop did not stock what he/she wanted.	Alternative product close (switch-selling).
Couldn't make up his/her mind.	More closely match his/her disclosed needs for a product.
Didn't like the colour scheme.	Order one in his/her colours, or mood-sell existing colours.
Was not attended to by an experienced seller.	Spot the problem and move in to take over the sale.
Was not attended to.	ditto.
'Just looking, not buying today.'	Ask questions to test his/her intentions.
'Better deal offered across town.'	Match the deal or concede add-ons.
'Want to think about it.'	Use the 'sooner or later' close.
'Can't afford that price.'	Offer loan finance.
Came in out of the rain.	If not busy, show them the range; if busy, hope it keeps raining.

| Got annoyed with the seller for some reason. | Review what went wrong and why; if somebody else responsible, bawl them out. |

Stores around the world spend almost as much training time on raising the percentage of viewers who buy as they do raising the amount they get from each buyer. Those that don't, won't survive. If 10 per cent more of the viewers buy something, and all buyers buy 10 per cent more when they do, then sales from the store will rise by more than 20 per cent, which in today's market is pretty good.

The 'cheap or low-cost' close

Probably the biggest problem in selling is overcoming a price objection. Now Slick has had a lot of practice in dealing with people who say 'the dishwasher is too expensive'. A strong hand for him to play is known as the 'cheap or low-cost' close. You need to be aware of what is happening when he gets to work on you.

Buyer: I like the dishwasher but it's too expensive.

Seller: Do you mean it costs too much or that its price is too high?

Buyer: Pardon?

Seller: You are obviously concerned with the price you pay for an *El Vigoroso* deluxe dishwasher, but have you considered the higher cost of the cheaper *El Limpo* washer?

Buyer: What do you mean?

Seller: Well, the price you pay to acquire a dishwasher reflects the quality put into the machine by the manufacturer. A washer, like the *El Vigoroso*, that is designed to last for years with virtually no servicing has a higher initial price than one, like the *El Limpo*, that is designed to survive its warranty but not much longer. The *El Limpo* will probably require regular servicing, which at today's service-call charges will cost £25 per visit plus parts, with any time longer than the first hour charged at £9 a quarter of an hour.

Buyer: Jesus, you must be joking.

Seller (slowly shaking head, with sympathetic facial expression to match – practised in bathroom mirror every morning): I wish I were, but some manufacturers only care about the initial sale price, and not about what it will cost the customer in the long run.

Buyer: And buying the *El Vigoroso* means I avoid all these horrendous service costs?

Seller: I can't say you'll *never* need a service call, only that it's most unlikely. I've not heard one of our customers complain about the reliability of the *El Vigoroso*. They pay a higher price initially but they are streets ahead in cost from then onwards. In fact, I can offer you at a discount an extra service-free warranty on the *El Vigoroso* we have in stock here – actually, this offer ended last week, but I'll put it through today for you if you order now and you promise not to tell my boss [slight conspiratorial nudge and a wink].

If you don't see what's coming next, you have not been paying attention. The buyer is about to stump up for the more expensive machine. But, you ask, is he wrong? Surely, Sid Slick had a point about the difference between cheap or low-cost?

Yes, indeed! And it is an important consideration for you when buying a domestic appliance, for there is nothing more frustrating than a stream of constant breakdowns that are unlikely to be cheap. Some warranties only cover for certain parts, not the expensive ones, and for limited amounts of labour time (the first hour, perhaps).

But the important point to note is that, while the 'cheap or low-cost' close might be an appropriate means for choosing between two appliances, it is not an appropriate means for deciding what to pay for the machine you decide to buy. That price – the list price – must be the subject of a separate negotiation:

Buyer: OK, suppose I was to choose the *El Vigoroso* – what special offers are available on it this week?

Seller: Well, I've already agreed to throw in the extended service-free warranty, and we do give a clock-radio with each purchase over £300.

Buyer: The extended warranty is nice, though if the machine is as reliable as you say that may not be worth much. I already have a clock-radio but I could use it as a Christmas present, I suppose. No, what I require if I am to buy the *El Vigoroso* today, is a 20 per cent discount, plus free delivery and installation in working order, and a supply of washing powders and rinse.

Seller: Phew! What are you trying to do, get me the sack?

Buyer: Not at all. I'm considering buying the *El Vigoroso*, but only if you help me do so.

Seller: Well, I can't cut the price by 20 per cent, nor can I get supplies of powder and rinse – what you see is all we have.

Buyer: How much will you take off the price, if I buy today?

Seller: Five per cent is all I have. Any more and we lose money.

Buyer (shuffling through brochures from other stores, and looking pointedly at a couple of pencil prices in the margins):   You must do better than that. I need 15 per cent off just to match the price quote I got on the phone from Wottadeal down the High Street. If we can't come to an equitable agreement, I'll try offering my business to Wottadeal.

Seller: Look, I'll tell you what. I'll take 10 per cent off the price, but that's my top limit, believe me. I'll throw in all the powders and rinse we have in the store, and we'll deliver and install it as well. You'll have to pay cash now, today, though. Now don't tell me that's not the best deal you'll ever get this side of the graveyard – where I'll probably end up once my boss sees what I've done.

Buyer: And the extended warranty and clock-radio?

Seller (laughing through clenched teeth):   What's your middle name – Scrooge? OK, it's a deal. Sign this order and go before I get the sack.

By separating the two decisions – which dishwasher to buy from how much to pay for it – you blunt the 'cheap or low-cost' close, and get a better deal. The method is the same no matter what appliances you are buying, and it also works for cars, yachts, office machines, computers and house extensions.

Just as Sid Slick's closes work on most customers most of the time – that's why he's called 'Slick' (his real name is Sidney Selmore) – so Superdeal counters work on him, most of the time. And if Slick won't do a deal (he misjudges your earnestness), it won't take long to find somebody else who will, such is the buyer's market you're in when you're firmly in the Superdeal driving seat.

Other closes

There are thousands of selling closes being used every day, in stores up and down the country. Handling a close requires experience, and some you'll only recognise *after* you get home and think about what happened to you in the store – that's how you get experience! Well-worn closes, like well-worn clichés, wear well because they work. You can learn to recognise them as soon as they get underway, inwardly groaning as you do when you hear a hackneyed one used by somebody who thinks you're hearing it for the first time.

The bagatelle close
In the bagatelle (as in a 'mere trifle'), Sid Slick diverts your attention from the total cost of the kitchen appliance to its much smaller cost per day, or per use.

Buyer: But at £52, the Fryalot electric chip fryer costs an awful lot of money.

Seller: I agree [they always agree, and then follow with a 'but'] *but* if you cook chips four times a week, as I think you said, and the fryer will last you for years – Fryalot Ltd guarantee their chippers for five years – you'll find that the real cost works out at less than 4p a fry, for the best deep-fried chips in the world! Can you honestly say that 4p is a lot of money? Your present chipper is probably costing you twice that, for less tasty chips. In fact, you're pounds ahead from the moment you buy the Fryalot.

Buyer: Well, putting it like that . . .

Seller: Are you paying cash or charge?

Slick has done it again! What can you get for 4p a throw today? It's a *mere bagatelle*. Yes?

The assumptive close
Once you have agreed the bagatelle, Slick throws in the *assumptive close*:

Seller: Are you paying cash or charge?

There are many versions, all ostensibly giving you a choice but, in fact, making the assumption on your behalf that you have decided to buy:

*   'Shall I wrap it or leave it in its box?'
*   'Shall we deliver it or do you want to take it away?'
*   'Which day is most convenient for you to take delivery?'
*   'Do you want the *ordinaire* version or the deluxe model?'

- 'What deposit would you like to pay?'
- 'Shall I put you down for twenty-four payments or eighteen?'

By answering any of these assumptive close questions, you confirm that you have decided to buy. The best response, if you haven't decided to buy, is some version of:

Buyer: I can only decide that when I've decided whether to buy or not.

This tells Slick that you have not yet agreed to buy and that he will have to do some more work on you (i.e. volunteer some more concessions, or be ready to agree to some you ask for) before he tries the assumptive close again.

The 'shame on you' close

All good sellers know that one of the most powerful selling closes is to play on the ego, or conscience, of the buyer. *They shame you into a 'buy' decision.* For this, they have to set you up first, and listen to whatever reasons you have for buying or to your responses to their prompting. It often works best when there are two of you buying together.

A familiar version plays to a sense of shame that you are not doing your best by your partner if you choose something other than the very best (and most highly priced) item in the range.

Doesn't she *deserve* the Prestige range of kitchen knives?

This is often used with jewellery and other expensive items, feminist protests notwithstanding!

Do you *really* let your man out without a Fryalot cooked breakfast?

Or, as it was done to me by a cousin of Sid Slick's:

Do you mean to say that you are willing to pay all this for a new kitchen and *not* put in a dishwasher?

When you hear the 'shame on you' close, turn off the buying urge; otherwise, he's got your measure and has found your 'buy button'. Keep in there for a deal:

She certainly does deserve the Prestige range of kitchen knives, but not at that price. Take 10 per cent off and I'll take them.

I'd be delighted to send him out with a Fryalot cooked breakfast, but unless you give me a discount for cash, I'm afraid we will have to get a set of Fryalot pans from Wottadeal instead.

I haven't agreed yet to pay any price for the new kitchen, but include a dishwasher, plus installation in working order, in your quoted price, and we might do business.

These counters use the 'shame on you' close to support your claims for a Superdeal.

You can do a reverse 'shame on you' on the seller:

You mean to say that having *almost* agreed to buy this complete set of kitchen appliances, you expect *me* to pay for installation?

Are you telling me that a company as well established as Fryalot does not automatically replace or repair faulty goods without a quibble?

The 'sooner or later' close

Many people survey the goods on display, and sometimes they listen to the seller's spiel and come close to saying 'yes'. Then something stops them – perhaps there's still a red light showing somewhere? – and they utter some version of the immortal lines:

I'd like to think about it.

I'll have to check with my wife/husband.

Sometimes this excuse is genuine, but in many cases, too numerous to count, this is another way of saying 'no' (as in 'Don't call us, we'll call you'). It's very difficult to say 'no' directly, even when pestered by somebody obnoxious. Women, though, have a lower 'no' threshold than men because they are more selective, and also they have to cope with many more obnoxious men than men have to cope with obnoxious women.

For Superdealers, it is always perfectly legitimate to want to think about a purchase before making one (exercising options and putting pressure on the seller). It is also the case that thinking about it often puts you off buying. Sellers know this and have developed several ploys to hold you in the store in the hope that you will decide to buy before you leave.

Among these, there is the 'sooner or later' close. This concentrates on your needs and how the appliance meets them:

Buyer: Well, thanks for your time, but I'd like to think about it before committing myself.

Seller: Of course you should think before making a purchase of this
          nature. You have agreed that the Doric freezer is large enough to
          meet your needs for storage, that it is within your intended
          budget, and that you need to solve the storage problem as
          quickly as possible. For you, it seems to me, there is one
          important decision: given your needs, how *soon* do you want the
          benefits of the Doric freezer to start working for you?

Buyer: As soon as possible. This problem is causing me concern, but I
          must think about a purchase of this size before going ahead.

Seller: Sure you must. The benefits from the Doric can be experienced
          by you sooner if you prefer, or later if you delay. You only pay the
          price once but you experience the benefits from the moment you
          own the Doric. Is there any benefit to you in delaying, when you
          can start experiencing the benefits immediately?

Depending on how you react, Slick might switch to a bagatelle
close (in response to your mention of a 'purchase of this size') or
continue reinforcing the message about experiencing benefits
sooner rather than later.

You can insist that you must think about it, perhaps by reference to somebody else that you must consult:

My partner will have to sign the order with me and he is in Hong Kong
until a week next Tuesday.

My wife/husband is not yet convinced that we have a problem, but I will
talk to her/him about it over the weekend and show her/him the
brochure.

Faced with a determination to leave and think about it, Slick has
to let you go, and put you down as saying 'no' politely. If you do
go back – and if he remembers you – he'll grin like a Cheshire cat
while he mentally spends his bonus again. Alternatively, if you
are ready to buy and Slick uses the bagatelle, you know how to
handle that to get a better deal.

Handling closes takes experience, but a little does go a long way,
for most people get worked over by them without knowing what
happened. Once you become 'close conscious', you'll spot them
coming and adopt appropriate responses that keep Slick's mind
on his need to improve his deal – if, that is, he wants to sell
anything to you on this occasion.

4

Coping with the workers

There never was a house that couldn't be improved, or didn't need some work done to it sooner or later. The men (and women) with the skills to undertake construction and house repair work of any kind are in a strong position when it comes to negotiating on price, quality and performance. This is reflected in the kinds of deals that most people make with them.

Superdealers approach the traumas of house repairs, conversions or extensions with a resolve not to be driven into near insanity, or alternatively near bankruptcy, by the loosely organised, though tightly priced, chaos that passes for the building industry. There are more rip-offs in this business than there are roofs in London, and you have to be wide awake to what is going on if you are to avoid being taken for a ride.

Almost worse than being taken for a ride is not getting anything started at all. You can wait months for something to start, longer for it to be finished, and still end up with a bodged up job that is almost as bad as what was there before.

A Superdeal strategy requires that you are in charge of what is happening, that you reserve your negotiating leverage (mainly by keeping your hands on your money until you are satisfied that the builders have done what they promised), and that you know what to avoid and what to insist on while coping with the wide variations in the quality (and to an extent, the honesty) of the people you'll meet who call themselves 'building contractors' and craftsmen.

Emergency house repairs

Before looking at major building work in your house, we shall consider some of the problems of hiring repairmen and others to do minor jobs about your property.

First of all, good ones are as scarce as an empty taxi in a rainstorm. With millions unemployed, it may seem amazing just how difficult it is to get a plumber, electrician, builder or decorator to actually turn up to give you a quotation for anything, and the small number who do are a crowd compared to the number who actually turn up to do the work!

In brief, their problem is that self-employed workers, and those employed in small businesses, are vulnerable to surges and ebbs in workloads. Much of the time, many of them do not have enough work to keep them busy. They get used to not working, and can hardly be bothered to do a small job, especially if it's an awkward one. Call on them during this phase and they don't bother to return your call, and if you do find them in, they don't come round when they have promised. Other times, they have more work than they have time for, and during this phase they still don't bother to return your calls and, if you find them in, they give you a date three months next Tuesday in the hope that you will go away with your tiresome little problem. In between these two phases, there is a narrow strip of time in which, if you call on them, they do call back, they do turn up and they do complete the job.

Getting to know some reliable craftsmen is a blessing to the householder, and their names should only be disclosed to the closest of one's friends (otherwise they get into a work surge just when you need them). Getting one to examine a proposal for some minor building or repair work is an achievement in itself – so much so, in fact, that many people disregard the cost in case an argument over price drives them back into their normal state of non-availability.

This is altogether a wrong approach. Superdealers look at the price negotiations with these people in the same spirit that they approach all disposals of their own money – that is, carefully – and they look for a better deal than the one the workman first thinks of.

There are several strands to the proper way to get property

repairs undertaken. First, let me dispose of the *emergency* repair.

Now, when you *need* a plumber, you really *need* a plumber, and when you need one, it's never at a time convenient to yourself. Leaks appear during the night, at weekends and during public holidays, seldom at other times; during weekdays, your plumbing system remains intact. Plumbers know this. Hence, in an emergency they generally find it easy to get premium rates for fixing things. This will happen to you too, if you come on in a panic.

To give yourself negotiating room, undertake some damage limitation – turn off the water taps, run off the tank into baths and so on. If the damage has been done already – you return to find your house like a scene on board the *Titanic* – don't jump to the phone at 2 am and call the 24-hour plumber in the Yellow Pages. If you do, he's gotcha.

After you have limited the damage to stop it getting worse, clean up as much as you can. There is nothing like a clean-up to put a problem in perspective, and to calm you down.

There is nothing you – nor the 24-hour plumber (it's not part of his service!) – can do about the damage that has been done. A ruined carpet stays ruined, a collapsed ceiling stays collapsed, a shorted electrical system stays dead, after the flood has hit them. The plumber will not put these right; he'll see you as a potential customer for the services of his mates – George the electrician, Fred the joiner, and Stan the plasterer – and if you panic enough, you'll probably agree to hire them (at premium rates).

What is the plumber going to do for you? Largely, repair the *cause* of the damage (but *not* the damage). Initially, however, he is called out to do what you can do for yourself – turn off the water – and give you professional sympathy at 2 am, and then he arranges to come back next day, or later if it's a Friday, to do the actual work. Meanwhile, it has cost you £40 for the night call-out. How much clearing up can you buy for £40?

What if the roof has blown off? There's not much he's going to be able to do for you during the night, is there? Even over a weekend, he's only going to do a holding repair, for it's likely that your insurance people will want to inspect the damage, assess their liability, loss adjust (i.e. adjust their liability for your compensation downwards) and give the go-ahead for the repairs.

Superdealers give themselves time to control the emotions

caused by the evident destruction of their property. They do not agree to premium rates in a panic. They call up plumbers during normal hours and get quotations for putting things right, or having established a good relationship with a local plumber, they ask him to call round and quote for the job.

When the plumber calls, the damage is limited, the area has been cleared up and the householder is calm and collected. Nobody is tear-stained and upset, and except for the leaking plumbing, there is an air of normality about the place. Now is the time for negotiations about the cost of doing the work.

Negotiating better deals with workmen

Repairs and improvements can either be handled by a local firm of contractors or by a self-employed workman. The choice is a matter of experience and convenience.

For anything relatively expensive, the quotations routine is probably the best approach. Always ask for more than one estimate. Ask three or more contractors to quote for the work, and then compare the quotes of those who bother to turn up. (If nobody turns up – a not-unusual event – keep ringing until somebody does.)

Comparing quotations involves more than looking at the price alone. A careful comparison of the statements of the work they will do for the money they are asking will show up differences in what is on offer. It is not always the case that the highest quote means that the most work will be done. Typically, there are things included in one quote that are not included in another, and these need have nothing to do with the total price to be charged.

The estimators who draw up quotations charge for the amount of labour and materials they think will be needed to do the job. They charge labour at its cost (to them) plus a mark-up (often 150 per cent) to cover their overheads, administration and profit for the job. They buy their materials from trade suppliers and, in their first quotation, often mark-up the costs to cover finance and the traditional 10 per cent for 'handling'.

All this is added together, with perhaps an allowance for any unforeseen contingencies (when they strip away the soggy plaster, they find new brickwork is needed), and is then presented as a quotation. Depending on how badly they want to do the work – they may have under-utilised workers in the yard – they pad or shave the price to suit.

It's now over to you.

No quotation is set in concrete. It is always padded, so challenge it! Because something is in writing, often in semi-formal language, it does not mean that it is immutable and cannot be amended as a result of your queries.

For example, in the case of a new bathroom, look carefully through the quotations – from Bathroom King, Tap Services and Design Suppliers – and write down what they are promising to do, paying special attention to the differences by making a list of which quotation is offering to do what.

NEW BATHROOM

Quote

All	Remove existing bath and replace with new bath:
BK	enamel bath
TS	composite bath, boxed in
All	Replace damaged tiles and render
BK	Retile walls to height of 1 metre
DS	Retile walls to height of 2 metres
All	Replumb bath
TS	Add bath shower taps
DS	Same and supply glass panels
BK	Same and supply smoked-glass panels
All	Replace existing sink
DS	Replace and box in sink
TS	Box in sink to match bath
All	Replace existing toilet
BK	Box cistern into window alcove
TS	Plumb in bidet
BK	Fit shaver point
TS	Fit medicine cabinet
DS	Same plus full-length mirror
All	Tile floor area
TS	Build step round bath

The differing prices they charge for their work are not important at this stage. *What you want is a new bathroom incorporating the best features of each company's quotation.*

Your list of demands, in the above example, might include:

Remove existing bath and replace with enamel bath, boxed in and replumbed, with shower attachment in working order, and fitted with smoked-glass panels.
Retile to 2 metres.
Replace sink and box it in same style as bath.
Replace toilet and box cistern into window alcove.
Fit shaver point over sink, with independent light.
Fit medicine cabinet.
Tile floor area in non-slip tiles.
Plumb in bidet.

These requirements exceed the quotation of any one company. Ask them to re-quote and see what they come up with. They might baulk at including all you ask for within their original price, but they might add some things to their original quote. If they do, you're ahead. If they don't, get more quotes based on your list. You will be surprised just how much can be added to a quote before the guy backs out. If he does, and you don't want to continue the search, give in on one item (the bidet? the boxing in? the tiling to 2 metres?), and see if that does the trick.

The idea is to level up the work content of the quotations and level down, or at least stay within, the prices originally quoted. The margins they work on give them room to do so, and the variety of their stocks in bathroom furnitures enables them to put together items to get to your price level.

All plumbers have loads of spare items – shower bases, shower taps, pipes, baths, toilets and bidets – and previously popular styles that they can use, if pushed, to get you a modernised bathroom at less than the price they first thought it would cost.

The same is true of kitchen, laundry, window and lighting suppliers and fitters. When they realise that you mean business, they meet you part way. True, they are used to dealing with customers who pay the first price they hear for the fashionable set of appliances they supply, but they know enough about their business to adapt to your requirements when you make their being met a condition of doing business at all.

How to use the Mother Hubbard

There are more rip-offs in new kitchens than you've had hot dinners.

The Freds of this world might build your kitchen, but it's the Adrians who 'design' it. If they capture your imagination, they are on their way to capturing a large slice of your income. And they have such helpful finance schemes available too!

Switch-selling is the most common technique in the new kitchens business. If Adrian can switch you up the range from three-ply to solid wood, he can treble or quadruple the extravagantly high price he quotes for the plywood job. If he can't, he still makes a whacking profit and you get a kitchen that gets shabby faster than your gardening boots.

The secret of switch-selling is to make you feel the cheapness of the shoddy. Adrian knows how to make you feel richer higher up his price range. The entry price of the cheap materials is shockingly expensive. They are meant to be, for the idea is to structure you into thinking big (in a money sense) about the cost of the home improvement. Adrian doesn't just have designs for your kitchen, he also has designs on your money.

The first question he asks is: 'How much are you budgeting for?'

If you disclose a figure well below his basic price, he tries to get you up to a reasonable (for him!) figure before he does any work; otherwise, he is wasting his time. Moreover, as pricing is not yet a science in business – 'what the market will bear' is the only rule – you can bet that, whatever kitchen you settle for, it will 'miraculously' cost your disclosed budget. Never in the history of kitchen design did anybody ever get change out of their budget for a new kitchen!

How should you handle this question? Don't commit yourself to anything. Get him to give you a rough quote for the design he has in mind, then try the *Mother Hubbard* (of the 'cupboard was bare' fame).

You know that whatever price he quotes you for a new kitchen is his best (for him) price, i.e. the one with the largest profit. In the Mother Hubbard you choose how bare to make the cupboard. If his first quote is £4000 and you only want to spend £3000, then tell him that your budget is only £2500. For a convincing Mother

Hubbard, you need a credible explanation as to why you only have £2500 available (it's all you have in the bank, it's all the bank will lend you, it's a small legacy) and a compelling reason why you cannot add to it at all (you're at your debt limit, etc.).

Adrian's sale is falling away before his eyes and he probably feels nauseous and his heart is pattering like a marathon runner's at the finish line. He can only retrieve the sale by finding a way to get down from the Everest price he had in mind. As his 'best' price is always a try-on, he has room to make cuts. If he believes that unless he gets down to your Mother Hubbard budget he isn't going to get a sale, and as his prices are padded, he can find a way to meet you, or get close enough to have a chance.

Suppose he comes back and says: 'I've cut everything to the bone, and it still comes out at £2800.' He might dress up his retreat by some minor amendments to the proposal. He thinks he is over your budget by £300, but you, of course, are now inside your real budget by £200. You can use that £200 to get back some of the quality he has cut out, and he can feel better about his retreat because he will think he has not given in totally.

When more than one company quotes, use the 'level up the proposed work for the same or lower price' routine described earlier. By working the Mother Hubbard in conjunction with a *Dutch auction*, at least in peripherals such as appliances and lighting, you are in the driving seat.

When the 'auction' stops – let them stop it, not you – place an order considerably below Adrian's opening price, incorporating the best ideas for your kitchen modernisation, with as many add-ons as you can get away with.

The underground economy

Although a lot of people pretend it doesn't exist, and many more shake their noble heads in disgust (at least in public), the fact is that there are a lot of people out there who have the skills, and often the tools, to carry out high-quality work on your premises at prices that defy common sense, unless you accept that they are working on the moonlit shift, on the 'q.t.', or while they are under some form of obligation elsewhere, such as on the dole.

Superdealers are sanguine about the underground economy. It

exists. It operates everywhere. It is a social phenomenon of our age, and it is none of our damned business. What people choose to do with their lives is their own affair. How they cope with the risks they take is up to them. Your concern is with your responsibilities and your life.

I know a car-hire firm that gets its Mercedes serviced by mechanics from the local Mercedes dealer – in the evening, on the quiet – for a fraction of the daytime price (that I pay!). I've heard of companies doing jobs for 'folding money' at half the price they normally charge, with no invoices, no receipts and no cheques.

A conversation could go like this:

Buyer: How much then for the window conversion?
Seller: £750, plus VAT.
Buyer: How much for cash?
Seller: What kind of cash?
Buyer: Folding money.
Seller: Will you be needing a receipt?
Buyer: Not at all. You do the job. When it's done, I pay you cash in used ten-pound notes, non-consecutive.
Seller: In that case, it will be £550, but give me back my written quotation.

Now, I know that of all the messages of *Superdeal* this one will draw the most comment from critics, some of whom are more sanctimonious than Holy Willie but with less justification (puzzled critics can refer to the poem by Robert Burns and recognise themselves). I am not recommending that you participate in the underground economy, nor am I moralising if you do, but there is clearly a lot of scope for getting household repairs done at a fraction (and a small fraction at that!) of the regular price.

Mainly the guys concerned are working for their labour time only. If they have a full-time job, or are on the dole, your payment is additional to their income, and they appear to value their own time much less than when they sell it to an employer, or would accept from the government. However, when they supply materials, they pay VAT to acquire them (the tax man gets something back), and when they spend their income from you, they pay VAT, excise duty and petrol tax; hence, the tax man gets yet more back. In many cases, if the underground workforce were not available, many people who avail themselves of its services would not do so, because the regular price is prohibitive. Its existence circulates money to a wider segment of the population than would otherwise benefit.

I will say no more, but as an economist, I know that my spending is your income, and you inevitably spend what you earn, and so it goes on. The tax man gets his cut in the end, no matter how anybody organises things. The folding-money brigade notwithstanding, taxation (like death) is certain.

Preparing for big jobs

Tackling a major building job, such as the complete renovation of an older building, or the conversion of a building from one use (e.g. place of worship) into another (place of abode), calls for considerable skills, both in conceiving the project (what you want done) and in arranging for the contractor to do the work to your satisfaction.

You are not just laying out your money; you are laying your sanity on the line. You can reduce (but not eliminate) the risk to your sanity only by increasing the cost by employing professional project managers (consultant engineers, architects) to undertake all of the work associated with design, specification, hiring contractors, negotiating prices and supervising the job through to completion.

This leaves the question: who supervises the project managers? Consultants are no more immune to idiotic decision-making than our friends in the real estate and legal business. If they get it wrong, there isn't much the builder can do to put it right except at additional expense. And if the consultant and the builder fall out over the blame for some defect or other ('who is blamed pays'), you can be left with a hole in the building in winter while they pursue each other through the courts or into arbitration.

Superdealers take a direct and personal interest in anything to which their money is pledged. When they use professional managers, they make sure that they and the managers think alike on every issue connected with a job. A thorough briefing, supported in writing by the most detailed of signed notes, forms the foundation of the relationship. Regular contact and consultation between the managers and the Superdealer characterises the nature of their partnership. The cash nexus does the rest.

It is *not* advisable to brief a consultant, hand everything over to him and then leave for three months' holiday in Clacton until the job is finished. You are likely to return to a building site, not a finished job, and if it is 'finished', it won't be the job you thought you had paid for.

First decide what you want done. Now this isn't easy, for your budgets chase the horizons of your wants more slowly than your horizons expand. You think you can do things to a building that would require more engineers than built the pyramids, and cost just about as much, too.

Imagination, however, is not a liability. Draw up your plans for the house using your imagination to the full. You can get all kinds of ideas out of the glossy magazines, not necessarily in a straight imitation of what you see but in a sensible adaptation to suit the structure of your building. List all the things that you would *like* to be included in the plans, room by room. Some of these may be the 'either/or' type ('either a door through to the diningroom, or a wall taken back three feet').

Now one thing is for certain: your list will be longer than anything your budget can remotely stand. So divide the list into two parts:

1. Changes I *must have*
2. Changes I would *like*

and then start a separate list of 'Features I *don't want*'.

The changes you *must have* are the basic structural changes you require for the building to serve its minimum purposes (whatever they are). They could simply be the complete replastering of all walls, the knocking through of some windows and doors, and the moving of a staircase. But without these *must haves*, the job is hardly worth doing.

Be warned: when it comes to the price negotiations, you will be pressed up against this minimum list, for everything in building costs more than you think (and even more if you do not prepare properly).

Changes you would *like* tend to be numerous. These are your add-ons, the delightful little bits that make your house near perfect in your imagination. It is right that you should list these, for if they can be undertaken in the major job, they should be, or, if not, having been once decided upon, they can become small projects for later when you and your cash balances have recovered.

The *don't want* list is useful for the architect, for he may be able to find ways of eliminating these from the building without necessarily having to compromise items from your 'like' and perhaps even your 'must have' lists. That, after all, is what he gets paid for: using proven professional skills to see things that we mere mortals miss.

Dealing with architects

At this point, consult an architect. There will be a charge for this initial consultation, and if he goes on to prepare drawings, his fee will be based on the RIBA (Royal Institute of British Architects) scale system based on the total price of the job.

Can you negotiate the scale fee? Probably not directly, though by deciding on the extent of the work, you raise or limit the architect's fee.

The recession has created many unemployed architects. I sip the odd glass of claret with several of them in my local wine bar, and I know, from listening to their tales of how they are 'getting by', that not a few hours a week are spent doing the odd creative job for this or that householder on the 'q.t.' at a fraction of the usual RIBA cartel-enforced fee.

Naturally, there are risks in using out-of-work architects. There are no come-backs if the building collapses, or the work does not meet planning regulations, which are as mysterious as the sex life of a hippopotamus. Architects in practice can be sued – you normally know where to find them – and some recompense might be secured for some of the damage. But you should remember that, while legal retribution, or the award of a professional arbitrator, might meet some or all of your financial losses, it will never be enough to compensate for all the indirect ones you suffer. Professional negligence is a risk no matter who you use, with slight odds favouring those in work, as those out of work might be in this sad state for reasons other than the ones they tell you.

Once detailed plans are agreed, check that all planning regulations are met. The consequences of slip-ups here are horrendous,
as planning officers are as ruthless at punishing an accidental
violation of their rules (for a start they don't believe there is such a
thing) as McEnroe is when served a loose ball. A consultation
with the local planning officers can be arranged on an informal
basis, and they can spot things quickly that need to be altered
before you submit the plans for official study. In my experience,
planning officers can be very helpful informally, though hell hath
no fury like a planning officer on the rampage when somebody
deliberately flouts the rules.

Dealing with builders

Your architect knows more about local builders than you do and
might recommend one or two to be approached for a quotation. If

not, get names from the Yellow Pages or from friends, and ask them to send round an estimator. Your detailed plans and specifications can be photocopied and handed to the estimators, and while doing this, you need not be shy about letting them know that they have competition.

Now you should know by this stage in *Superdeal* that the price they first quote to you is the best price for them, not necessarily for you. They estimate the labour time involved and price it, plus a mark-up to cover overheads, administration and profit. They also charge the materials to you at the cost to them from their suppliers, plus another mark-up.

Anything they handle as a middle-man between you and the original supplier attracts a mark-up of at least 10 per cent, including all fittings and fixtures for the property (door handles, rails, doors, window frames, etc.). They also add something for contingencies – unforeseen extras that become apparent during the job. Sometimes they invent contingencies because they have an allowance for them.

You need to check their quotations very carefully as the English language is sometimes misleading: 'installation' may not include 'making good' the plastering work unless it specifies this; fitting lights to ceilings likewise can leave small holes or at least a mess; knocking a hole through for a window might leave out the cost of the window frame and so on.

Make sure they include the removal of all rubble, etc., but check what happens to valuable scrap such as copper pipes, lead linings and so on. If they are 'allowing' for the scrap price in the quote, insist that they estimate how much the scrap is worth. If they don't mention the fate of valuable scrap, insist that they credit you with the price they obtain, or dispose of it yourself. Workmen sometimes kid you that the scrap is theirs 'tradition-ally'. That's rubbish. Start a new tradition or, better still, hold the scrap back until a little 'extra' needs doing and 'pay-off' the builders with it.

Compare each quotation for the work they say they will under-take and the price they want to charge for it. Here the procedure is the same as for a smaller job: *level up the work; level down the price*.

Draw up a list of all the best features of each quotation – the composite work list – and run through a 'Dutch auction' sequence for as long as they will play, for those items that are worth including in the finished job.

Be warned: don't get too greedy. Builders have ways of getting back at you if they are squeezed too hard: poor workmanship, shoddy materials, bad timekeeping, loose ends left for weeks and a general campaign of near sabotage by the use of the 'buggeration factor' (basically, the myriad ways that are available to screw up a job and drive the client slowly insane). Your architect can be valuable in advising you what to go for, by tempering your boldness with just enough modesty.

Two ways of hiring workmen

A major job can be undertaken by using a single contractor or by employing one contractor for the majority of the work supported by finishing trades to complete it. There are advantages and disadvantages in both methods.

A single contractor takes responsibility for the whole job, right through to live-in-standard decorating. He coordinates all the different workers, schedules their work and supervises its continuation and completion.

Firms big enough to employ full-time in-house skilled craftsmen to cover every trade used in building work are often 'top heavy' with managers and administrators. You pay for them and their Rolls Royces, as well as for overheads you never use and never see, and equipment they never use and stores they have over-ordered. If it's a family business, you pay for the son's lifestyle too – and there's always a son, part wastrel, part know-all and generally part-time too.

The building trade is notorious for its ups and downs (and for many builders, there are more downs than ups). The full-time employee is expensive, and not just because of his wages. He cannot always be kept busy enough to justify these, but by charging out his labour – and often exaggerating the hours he works for you – the builder can keep him on the books until the boom returns. You pay for that.

Some large firms compromise and employ a core of full-time skilled workers who have just enough to keep them busy (paid for by you), and they hire extra men, who usually work on their own account, as and when they need them for specific jobs such as wiring, plastering, tiling and plumbing. This arrangement does not save you anything because you are charged the usual overhead rate on labour no matter what its employment status. If the in-house labour is charged to you at £20 an hour – to pay for the company Rollers and their top-heavy administration – the freelance labour is charged at the same rate, even though they are paid, say, £10 an hour, with the builders pocketing the difference. It's worth it to builders to hire casual skilled labour in this way, for they don't have to pay wages when there is no work, and it's very profitable to do so when they are working, as the mark-up can be skimmed off.

On the other hand, using a main builder to do the core work only – structural re-arrangements, etc. – and hiring your own skilled individuals for specific tasks (rewiring, plastering, plumbing, painting, and cosmetic rather than structural joinery) can save you between 15 and 20 per cent on a big contract. I had a bathroom tiled by a tiler who I thought was an employee of the main contractor until he handed me his card and told me it was cheaper to hire him direct. Hence, in later jobs, I did.

With regard to the underground economy, you may well be able to save even more (30 to 60 per cent) if you can hire your skilled men from the apparently endless stream of willing workers who surface regularly in the twilight world of 'folded money'.

Whichever way you hire your labour to supplement the core work completed by the main builder, it calls for an increase in your supervisory involvement in the project, which can be time-consuming. It also makes you vulnerable to 'games' played when each new set of workers complains loudly about the state in which the previous lot left their share of the job. Sometimes they indulge in a direct try-on to see if you will pay their pals to re-do the allegedly awful work not 'properly done' by the people you paid off yesterday. If you know some good people who don't cheat, you won't face this nonsense. Otherwise, it's down to your judgement as to their honesty – a notoriously difficult and imprecise business, even for cynics!

Superdealers search for the lowest-cost way of getting a quality job done. I think labour charged to you by a major contractor is the most expensive way of getting a job done. Hence, I favour the second option: a major builder for the structural work; individual craftsmen for the finishing and decorative work.

Avoiding the 'extras'

When you choose a contractor (Droppa Brick Ltd), there are some things you must watch out for.

You need to agree a properly sequenced work timetable. Jobs that take 'five to six weeks' invariably take eight; 'two to three months' means five, etc. If you let them get away with a vague promise to undertake the work as best as they can, they are sure to take their time about it. Also, a contractor who is vague in timing is generally lax in quality control. Insist on a timetable in writing and check it each time there is a slide in a deadline (as there will be, as sure as builders go bust).

Fix firmly the means by which you pay for the job, bearing in mind that work paid for in advance tends to encourage the work to be done in arrears, if at all. I know a guy who paid in advance for a roof to be built over his patio: three years later, he still has a roofless patio! So never agree to payments in advance. A builder who wants payment in advance is probably going bust and it's better for you that he goes bust without your money.

An agreement for regular payments on completion of scheduled bits of work is far better for you than one for weekly payments for whatever work they do. Builders and others have a habit of disappearing to do rush jobs elsewhere, or to go to the betting shop, etc. They prefer to be paid by the hour which gives them scope for dragging out the time they take to do a job; you prefer to pay for the job being completed in the agreed time. Hence, when, say, a wall is removed and replaced to the architect's or your satisfaction, you pay them, but not before. If the work falls behind because of slack supervision, that is a cost to the builder who is kept waiting for his money, and not to you because you hold the money until he stops keeping you waiting for the job to be finished.

It is customary in large contracts for clients to *hold back* a percentage of the contract value for some weeks after a job is done – on a hydroelectric scheme worth millions of dollars, the client may hold back about 5 per cent for a year or more. When clients really wish to turn the screw, they require contractors to deposit large 'performance bonds' with them. These can be cashed on demand by the client if the contractor's performance falls below par, in the opinion of the client, not the contractor. The holdback clause ensures that defects that surface after the builder has allegedly finished are fixed promptly and with goodwill, and you don't have to do a version of a break dance in their office just to get their attention.

I recommend the holdback clause for rewiring jobs, for example; there's nothing like blue flashes at rewired switches for frightening the cat, and the holdback ensures they are fixed on request and at no extra charge. You should apply the holdback to any major building job. It is an accepted practice in the business, though it is not offered without prompting.

Another dodge Droppa Brick Ltd will try in order to boost their profits (and to make their quote look more attractive) is to quote for the work to be done plus the basic materials and, in addition, also quote purely nominal costs for all the fittings your job requires. Ostensibly this gives you the choice of paying more for a higher quality than for the basic standard. The problem comes from you thinking only of the choice you have been given, and not of the cost of that choice and how it is arrived at.

Droppa Brick sends you along to the retail counter at the suppliers they recommend, and you choose the doors, tiles, baths and windows you want from the extensive range on display. The cost of these is bound to be higher than the nominal cost they allowed for in their quote because anything other than war surplus (Boer, not Vietnam) works out to cost about ten times what has been nominally allowed. The fittings are sent to the builder's yard to await delivery to your house when they are needed, and your builder adds their 'usual' mark-up to the *retail* price in your account. Droppa Brick, of course, buys all the fittings you order, not from the retail counter where you chose them, but from the trade counter at the same supplier (it's usually round the side of the building, where the vans are kept – you'll park next to the Volvos in the retail shop area).

Superdealers, however, get control of these costly items (do you know off-hand the cost of a door, or the price of enough tiles to cover a small wall?) by ignoring the retail counter and going to the trade counter (not in a three-piece suit!) at the same supplier. If he asks (which is unlikely), tell Stan, the trade-counter manger, that you are from Droppa Brick Ltd, which is approximately true as your order will be delivered to them and charged to their account. Order the items you want, noting down their trade prices, which Stan will give to you (he only keeps these prices from the 'mugs' who buy retail!).

Accurate information is ammunition!

Tell Droppa Brick that you did as they suggested, but add that you checked the trade prices – 'in case Droppa Brick are overcharged by Tom & Jerry Supplies'. Naturally, Droppa Brick will get the real message: you know the true price of your fittings, and this limits their ability to overcharge you for them.

In these circumstances, it is unlikely that they will charge you at retail prices, or put on a mark-up. (They might ring Stan at Tom & Jerry Supplies' trade counter and tell him he's off Droppa Brick's Christmas gift list!) If they do try to charge you some weeks later, remind them of the trade prices you checked and tell them to correct their oversight. Any spluttering justification they give for the rip-off will die to a whimper by the time you settle the account.

Changing your mind

A word on 'extras' that are caused by you changing your mind. Mind changes in the building and construction business are as common as broken brick and they provide a lucrative side-line for many a builder. No matter what they may say, they just love clients who tell them to knock down a wall they have just put up, or to move a door six inches to the left.

Why?

Because whenever clients change their minds, the cash register keeps on ringing. There is the charge for doing the job one way, and the charge for undoing the job, before charging you for doing it another way.

I once advised a firm of consulting engineers on training their site engineers to negotiate payments for the changes their clients were making to buildings during construction. The company reckoned it was costing them their profits on each job because their site engineers usually agreed to expensive changes without charge. Your smaller builder does not need my services in this area: they are experts at clawing back money for the most minute changes:

Phew. You mean you want to have the light switch two inches lower? That's a lot of work, madam. I'll see what I can do but we put it where the plans said it was to go. I'm afraid I'll have to make a charge for the extra work, and I'll need to sweeten Fred's redoing it with some overtime. OK?

The cheapest way to avoid charges for changing your mind is not to change your mind once the plans have been approved. This, however, is not always possible. New ideas come to the surface when you see the possibilities created by rebuilding work – space appears that you did not think you had.

I had a bath moved forward 15 centimetres and discovered that the space behind it was just (within 1 cm) big enough for a separate shower unit, but some of the new plumbing work at the head of the bath would need to be redone. The problem: how to get this done without being charged the earth?

First, I did not ask them: 'How much would you charge for putting in a shower unit and redoing the bath plumbing?' That would give them ideas they might not have at that precise moment. You never know, perhaps the plumbing needs to be redone because it has not passed the foreman's inspection, and they were going to redo it anyway.

Instead, I asked the foreman for his opinion on whether a shower unit could be installed beside the bath. He offered the view that it could but not as a standard shower fitting:

I have a shower base – solid porcelain – in the yard that we had left over from a job at the hospital. I'll give you that for nothing. You will have to buy some shower fittings but we'll forget about the replumbing work. We'll tile it at cost but you pay for the joinery work to box it in.

The result: a first-class improvement to a bathroom for £80 instead of £200, which added many more pounds to the value of the house, and a lot of convenience to the family.

Hence, *don't offer to pay for a change of mind in your building project; wait for them to price it.* If they want to do it at full cost – plus expensive fittings – see if you can get them to use less expensive materials, or surplus fittings, and try for 30 per cent off the price as a matter of course. If you're offered 15 per cent, you're well ahead.

Your checklist

- In quotations, level up the work, level down the price.
- Use the Mother Hubbard to pull down a padded quotation.
- With bigger jobs, take a personal interest in the project.
- Consider offering 'folding money' to cut a price.
- Prepare for a bigger job by stating what you *want*, what you'd *like* and what you *don't want*.
- Check that the architect's detailed plans accord with the planning regulations.
- Check a builder's quotation very carefully for assumptions about what they are actually offering to do for the money.
- Decide whether you want a main contractor or a contractor and labour-only sub-contractors.
- Insist on a work schedule for the job and pay only for work done, not for hours 'worked'.
- Use trade counters to acquire fittings and check the prices.
- If you change your mind during the project, do not offer to pay for the changes – let them suggest a price and then negotiate it downwards.

5

Buying and selling houses

In general, only the very poor and the very rich rent their houses; the poor because they must, the rich because they can. Most of the rest of us own our houses, and, apart from the bounty of inheritance, to own one we have to buy one. (By 'house' I mean any dwelling place – house, flat, bungalow, caravan, castle, etc.)

A house is probably the most expensive purchase and largest sales transaction you will ever make on your own behalf, and if your job or circumstances force you to buy, sell and buy again and again, going about it in a Superdeal way helps you to do better each time.

For first-time buyers, the entire business can be perplexing. Just moving house puts your ticker under great stress and can be a severe test for your marriage, your friendships and even your sanity (hence, try to avoid changing any three of the following at the same time: your job, spouse, house, politics and sex).

Why is buying or selling a house so stressful? It may be because you think it is going to be easier than it turns out, sometimes because you believe that the person with the money is in a stronger position than the person with the bricks (or vice versa). But when you hear from the owner of a house that several people are clamouring to buy it (I've never heard a seller tell anybody otherwise), or from a buyer that other houses for sale that week do not need expensive work to make them habitable (may you always deal with buyers who praise your house and warm to your price), you can leap from 'normal' to 'neurotic' faster than a Ferrari goes from 0 to 60, and whatever else you feel – probably a mixture of nausea and numbness – you no longer feel so confident. If the search for a new house, or the wait to sell your old one, has been a long one, physical exhaustion is added to the weariness of your spirit, and like a dehydrated traveller in a desert who perceives a mirage, you will believe in the favourable features of almost any house brought to your attention by estate agents Messrs Slum, Ghetto & Blight, or the sincere qualities of any buyer they introduce to you.

It need not be like this. You can buy a sound and safe house within your means and which suits your needs, or sell your house for a price to make the hassle worthwhile, if you go about it in a sensible Superdeal way.

To start, we must admit that not all houses are safe and sound. Some buildings – part of the Lord's wider plans for the universe – are held together in defiance of the known laws of science. You won't know this until after you have bought the property – nothing falls down in the building business until after you have paid for it (the original example of Murphy's law – he probably built it!)

Moreover, not all people selling houses are candidates for a heavenly reward in the hereafter. In fact, you might as well start from the position that *all house sellers are liars*. That way you won't be surprised to hear from the seller more than a few of what Winston Churchill called 'terminological inexactitudes'. Honesty is a commodity in greater evidence from sellers when it costs them nothing; the higher the cost of honesty – the loss suffered from telling the truth – the less inclined are sellers to be honest about their properties. They may not directly lie to you – they may just miss out a few things by omission, and your surveyor may miss them too, especially if it is Mr Nearsight, the senior partner from Damnquick & Expensive, doing what he laughably calls a survey.

Finding a safe and sound property (in both a physical and a legal sense) is only one in a long chain of steps, each of varying length and complexity.

The opportunities to pay a higher price than the lowest the seller would have accepted are more numerous than is conducive for a good night's sleep. You need your wits about you when negotiating with the likes of Mr Ivor Bettaoffer, and his partner, Mrs Notta Quidless, from Messrs Slum, Ghetto & Blight.

To buy a house, you have to have the finance, and there are a lot of expensive ways to borrow money, whether it be by a mortgage from a building society or a loan from a bank or against an insurance policy, or from the builder of the house. But the most expensive way of all is to offer too much for the house. That forces you to finance a higher loan than perhaps you can afford, or to do without other things you could have bought if it wasn't for the additional monthly repayments. Also, lenders might have more sense than you when they see the valuation report and compare it with the price you have agreed to pay; this could force you to use up more of your own capital to cover the difference between the loan they will give you on that house and the purchase price you rashly offered for it.

The completion date may never materialise if you get 'gazumped' by the seller. Here, the English system exposes you to the risk that, before contracts are exchanged, sellers can accept an offer from some other buyer, even though they have accepted a deposit and have agreed to sell a house to you. Fortunately, an offer to buy in Scotland has the full force of a binding contract on both parties from the moment it is accepted by the seller, hence gazumping is rare because the seller is in peril of legal retribution.

There is, of course, nothing that you can do about gazumping (except have a good cry), though I don't doubt that Messrs Waist, Phee & Sue will gladly take your money in a forlorn chase for compensation from the perfidious seller who gazumped you. *(For the alternative way of looking at gazumping, see below.)*

When selling a house, you might as well start from the point of view that *all house buyers are thieves*. Give a buyer half a reason and he will chop hundreds, nay thousands, off your price. Their sharpsighted surveyors, Messrs Alert, Forewarn & Prudence, don't miss a thing: they can spot a camouflaged repair job at ninety paces.

There is no law that says you must get the price you want, or need, for your house. The buyer has to agree to your price, otherwise it's 'bye, bye' not 'I'll buy'. You could accept a price much lower than the one your valuer told you the house is worth, or one much lower than the buyer was prepared to pay. But the most expensive way to sell a house is to sell it cheap. Such folly forces you into borrowing more for your next house.

You can't be sure that the buyer, having made you an offer, will stick to it. He might try the 'surveyor's lament': 'My offer was subject to survey and your house didn't make it.' He could also embrace you in a buying chain, with nothing settled for months and the risk of a 'collapse' of one of the links at any moment. If the delays are inordinate, you could lose the customer you thought you had and meanwhile turn down customers who were ready to buy. Thus, gazumping becomes an attractive short cut, not necessarily for any extra money that might be on the table, but to get the deal completed, and therefore, whatever your conscience, self-interest dictates that you gazump.

How to win in the house market

To win in the house market, you need to sort out your ideas before you start. Whether you are buying or selling a house, your attitude and thinking are your main assets or your largest liabilities. This is the biggest transaction of your life, and you want to get it right. So before we walk through a house negotiation, let's check that we are talking the same language.

Let's consider some principles that might save you a fistful of pound notes. Keep them handy when you are in the house market, and glance at them, just before you walk up a path to look over a house, or just before you answer the doorbell for a couple of viewers.

The other guy doesn't give a damn about you. Sure, the seller grins like a Cheshire cat, but most sellers grin by instinct and the rest by grooming. The sweet old lady showing off her house, smiling and coo-ing about this or that wonderful feature, is actually a wolf in drag. She might look like Red Riding Hood's granny, but her only object is to get rid of her house as quickly as possible to the person who pays the highest price. Having accomplished the sale, she will take herself off elsewhere without any concern for you. You may think I am overly cynical, and not a little cruel to Red Riding Hood's granny, but I don't care if the sellers are candidates for sainthood: if they are selling houses, they are as likely to lie as the most obvious of crooks, except the crooks are obvious and they are not!

Sure, the buyers on your doorstep are ultra-polite and listen to everything you say with an earnestness reserved for gossips, but the fact remains that buyers do not give a damn about you either, and if they buy, they hope never to see you again. The nice couple you are showing round your home who pretend to be unimpressed with every feature in it are on a moral plane with Bonnie and Clyde: privately, they adore your house and will pillage their entire repertoire of ploys to buy it off you for as little as you can be persuaded to part with it (and less, if they can).

The lesson: Superdealers do not get emotionally involved either with what they are buying or selling, or with the people with whom they are doing business. The benefit of an arm's-length relationship with the other guy is largely one of self-protection. You have no reason, other than wishful thinking, to take a stranger into your confidence, and by refraining from forming illusions that the other guy is a new-found friend, you will not make the mistake of disclosing to him relevant facts about your negotiating position. This leads straight to the basic truth about the balance of power in a negotiation, well understood by Superdealers.

As it is not obvious who needs the deal most, buyers who disclose their enthusiasm or, worse, their desperation to buy a house will always pay more than those who don't; and sellers who disclose a deadline or, worse, their desperation to sell, will always get less for their house than those who don't. No seller ever lowered his price because he learned that the buyer was enthusiastic, and no buyer ever raised his offer because he found out about the desperate plight of the seller. You have no way of knowing from a casual visit which of you most needs to complete the deal – the seller might be absolutely desperate and ready to drop on price . . . until, that is, you start disclosing your own urgent needs, at which point, new life starts pumping round the seller's nether regions and a smell of a sale at a higher price invades his nostrils.

Do not disclose any information about your needs to sell or buy, no matter how pressing your need is or how horrendous the consequences if you don't. The other guy may be desperate too, but he will be sharp enough to overcome his own worries with a worse offer for you if he thinks you are on your last legs.

There is no such thing as 'the house you must have'. If you don't get the one you want today, another, better one will turn up on the market tomorrow.

Not being clear on this point causes people to offer well over the odds for the house they fall in love with, and when it comes to putting a ceiling on what they can offer to get it, they have less sense than a sixteen-year-old in the torments of a first passion.

No matter how much you are under time pressure to buy or sell a house, you never need to buy a house so badly that you buy the wrong one, or sell one so cheaply that you practically give it away. The house market can be expected to take up a lot of your time. Because it is the biggest transaction that you will handle, it ought not to be rushed.

Circumstances can sometimes almost cripple you with press- ure – you're in debt, you've changed jobs, your spouse has left you or is about to do so, the family is crammed into a hotel room or, worse, they are squatting with relatives, you live a long way from your new location, you can't afford where you are now and the bank is lining you up for foreclosure and so on. Buying the wrong house, however, is never a solution to the severest of these pressures, because the stress of living in the wrong house and knowing that you made that kind of mistake is never worth the relief of having bought something at last.

In the same way, selling cheap is no solution to your problems. If you are in debt, selling cheap is an expensive way to get out of it and hardly qualifies you as a safe person to handle money and assets. You can recover from debts, even big ones, but doing an *el cheapo* only postpones alterations to your bad financial habits. You can only rectify a wrong decision by a correct one and you might as well get it right the first time, not only to save you the grief involved, but also the added expense.

Bear these principles in mind and save yourself a lot of worry and stress. Ignore them and you'll know the difference.

What you need to know

No negotiator can do too much preparation. The bigger the deal, the more detailed and thorough the preparation. Lots of people buy and sell houses with less thought than they choose partners, causing almost as many changes of partners as there are house sales.

Unfortunate house choice probably accounts for a large proportion of the divorce rate – Aphrodite or Adonis would be sorely tested as partners if you expected them to share a dank, dismal, and dingy cellar behind the gasworks. A lousy house sale, which can hardly be hidden from your partner, is going to cause emotional stress. Few people respect somebody they regard as responsible for squandering their share of the main (only?) asset they own.

The following points should be the *minimum* you should consider before proceeding:

To buy a house, you must:	*To sell a house, you must:*
1. Decide on where you want it located.	1. Establish its value.
2. Calculate your cash maximum.	2. Choose a price range.
3. Search the market.	3. Prepare it for sale.
4. Discover what's wrong with the house you choose.	4. Market it.
5. Agree a price with the seller.	5. Agree a price with the buyer.

There are no tricks for getting your preparation right other than that you should spend some time thinking about it.

Only you can weigh up the options to suit you and your partner, for if you choose wrongly, in your own or your partner's estimation, you will have to live with the choice and perhaps without your partner.

How to prepare to buy

Location
Location depends on personal choice and circumstance. One consideration is the cost of locating some distance from your place of work. Commuting costs are only avoidable if you live close to your job. You don't need a degree in urban geography to know that locating nearer the centre of a town raises the price you pay for your house, while reducing the cost of getting to work. There are also trade-offs between a larger, more roomy house in the country, and a smaller, more compact apartment closer to town.

One way to sort out your preferences when you have several conflicting options available, or you can't agree with the other people involved, is to list on a sheet of paper *all* the local features of specific locations – access to shops, schools, pubs, main roads, bus services, parks, countryside, commuting costs to work, size of garden, future developments, noise levels of traffic, aircraft and nearby factories, etc. – that are important to you all and rate them on a scale from 1 to 5 in increasing order of value.

CHOOSING A LOCATION

1 = awful; 2 = poor; 3 = average; 4 = good; 5 = excellent

Feature	House A	House B	House C	House D
Shops	....	....	....	....
Schools	....	....	....	....
Parks	....	....	....	....
Transport	....	....	....	....
Roads	....	....	....	....
Services	....	....	....	....
Amenities	....	....	....	....
Pubs	....	....	....	....
Work	....	....	....	....
Traffic	....	....	....	....
Distance from work	....	....	....	....
Distance from relatives	....	....	....	....
Other	....	....	....	....
Totals	_____	_____	_____	_____

Highest scorer: House ... = the preferred location

A perfect match with a preferred feature would score 5, a poor match 1 or 2. Some houses will score higher in some respects than others, but when you add up the total scores for each house, you can see if there is a clearly preferred location given the features that you have chosen for your comparison.

Your cash maximum
Houses sell for cash. It is the cash price that buys the house, not your monthly payments, and it is a common mistake to confuse what you can afford in monthly payments with the total price you pay for a house. Put simply, *there is no advantage to you in being able*

to afford the monthly payments if you agree to pay a ridiculously high price for a house. Not that any seller will contradict your view that it is the instalments that count and not the price you pay.

Mass-market builders (and car dealers) often attract buyers by emphasising the *low* cost of their monthly payments, while downplaying the total price that actually has to be paid: 'You can own this three-bedroom semi and move in Saturday for only £49 a week.' They also offer 'free' fitted carpets, curtains and kitchens, as well as 'free' videos, colour TVs, holidays in Spain, etc. What they don't tell you is that the price of a house you are buying for 'only £49 a week', has been increased by several thousand pounds to pay for the 'extras' you are supposedly getting for free. When you come to sell the house, you'll find that the price you paid to buy it a year or so earlier is still grievously higher than the price you can sell it for.

How then do you calculate your cash maximum?

That depends on your circumstances, but in all cases you will have buying costs (valuation and structural survey fees, conveyancing charges, legal fees, insurance premiums and taxes) and these must be allowed for in calculating your cash maximum, i.e. the price you can afford to pay for a house.

First-time buyers almost always rely entirely on a small cash deposit (their savings), plus what they can borrow from a bank or building society. After taking account of their buying costs, this sets the maximum cash price they have available to buy a house. (*See* Chapter 11 for the ways a Superdealer can get more out of a bank or building society.) Home owners, on the other hand, can realise some or all of their equity in the old house and apply it to the new purchase. Equity is the difference between the price you get for your house and any loans outstanding on it. Your equity, plus what you can borrow, minus your buying costs, is your cash maximum.

The amount that you can borrow is closely related to your ability – though, alas, not your intention – to pay it back. Your income must be sufficiently high to pay the interest charged against your loan, and also pay back the money you borrowed within the agreed time period (usually twenty or twenty-five years).

Broadly speaking, a reputable lender (bank or building society) will lend you up to three times the main income in the family plus any secondary income. Sometimes you can do better than this (3.5 times the main salary plus 1.5 times the secondary salary), and sometimes slightly worse (2.5 times the main salary and nothing at all for the secondary income). Home loans are negotiable, dependent on your personal circumstance, the lender's (not your) view of your risk worthiness and the state of the economy. Hence, if you earn £12,000 and your partner earns £8,000 a year, you could be eligible to borrow between £30,000 and £54,000 as a house mortgage. What the lender will actually offer you against a particular house purchase will depend on the surveyed condition of the house as well as the vetting of your status.

Finding out your *maximum* borrowing ability before you begin looking at houses helps you to keep a sense of proportion and avoid disappointments. You can shop around banks, building societies and endowment brokers to see just how much you can borrow. Add this amount to any other sources of cash available for house purchase (again, don't forget your buying costs – valuers, solicitors and tax collectors are not among nature's most patient of creditors!).

Searching the market
This figure – your cash maximum – sets the price range in which you search the market for your house. That is, of course, assuming you can keep your head when all around you are losing theirs: spouses expect you to go over budget whenever they fall in love with a house – no spouse ever fell in love with a house within a cash maximum. The problem is psychological: no matter what your cash maximum, the houses you can afford you don't fancy, and the ones that you fancy you can't afford.

Superdealers believe it is far better to attack the seller's asking price, before they succumb to demands to go above their cash maximum.

Think of it as El Dumpo *(discovering what's wrong)*
Why *El Dumpo*? Because if you don't get control of your emotions, you will surely fall in love with a house and pay more for it than you should.

There is a momentum in the buying of houses that, if not controlled, leads you to rush to purchase. And one thing is absolutely certain in any business: hot buyers pay more than cool buyers, and they regret their purchases even faster than they make them.

Buyers of houses often experience an emotional surge that impels them to say 'yes' when, in fact, they should either say nothing or, if pressed, 'maybe'. In almost all cases, the impulse buyer, or somebody buying under great time pressure, forgets to appraise the property as *El Dumpo* and keeps seeing it as *El Magnifico*, and this is fatal to good sense.

To protect yourself, go round any likely house with a determination to find things wrong with it. List everything that is out of order, plus any negative features you can find: woodwork that is split, doors that don't fit, handles that are slack, paintwork that needs redoing, tiles that are askew, ceiling and wall stains of any kind, taps that are dripping, heating that looks tired, windows that are small or don't open easily or are draughty, views that are blocked, gardens that are too large/too small/need attention/look difficult to manage, rooms that look crowded, cupboards that are full, and lofts that are not insulated (or if they are, they need four not two inches).

Remember that, in any house you are thinking of buying:

- No rooms are 'large'. They are *always* smaller than you expected. The smallest bedroom is a 'boxroom' or 'large cupboard'; ditto the study; and the diningroom is too small for your large antique table.
- No view is 'super' or 'magnificent'. It is always not worth commenting upon (if you do so, they've 'gotcha').
- No woodwork is 'beautiful'. It is a dust trap ('how difficult is it to keep clean?').
- No kitchen is 'fitted'. It's squeezed into a small space, and it always has something you want missing from it: dishwasher, hob units, disposal units, double sink, more cupboards, more plugs, room for the freezer, etc. ('We just have to have somewhere to put our dishwasher, darling' is a useful bit part for your spouse.)
- No bathroom is complete without a separate shower ('where can we put the bidet?'), floor-to-ceiling tiles, room for a jacuzzi, full-length mirrors, etc. If it has these: 'we really need two, even three or more bathrooms.'
- No garden is 'just right'. It's always 'just wrong': too large/too

small; too much lawn/not enough; no room for vegetables/ too much; no room for the kid's pool/a pool is too dangerous; too open/too sheltered; too much work/hardly worth the effort; and so on.

- No garage is large enough, in the right place, compatible with the house design. Alternatively in the absence of a garage, it can't be done without and will have to be built.

Get the idea? You are protecting yourself by deliberately practising finding faults.

Taking some trouble here to make out a list, and making it obvious that you are doing so, helps to structure (downwards) the seller's expectations of the market price of the house. Loosen the seller's attachment to the price he first thought of – which means persuading him that he is being unrealistic, or, alternatively, not saying anything at all that can reinforce his belief in his price – and you are more likely to pay less for it.

You can assume that all defects will be ignored (if not absolutely denied) by the seller. As they are unlikely to draw your attention to flaws that might put you off buying, you must closely look for them yourself. There are exceptions to this, however. A couple once magnanimously drew my attention to a seriously cracked wall in their house and produced three builders' estimates for putting it right. I have also been shown a house that had a sloping floor, which the owner claimed was my imagination, until I let gravity roll a ten-pence piece from the door to the window.

Finding a lot of defects and flaws might save you a lot of trouble if it persuades you not to buy the house at all. That is a better frame of mind to be in than its opposite: 'ooing' and 'aahing' at every new revelation of the house and its wonders. It is absolutely imperative that you do not appear keen (let alone *too* keen) on a house. In your mind's eye, it is *El Dumpo*! Don't let the seller sense that he owns *El Magnifico* as this will only encourage him to be firm on his price.

How to take on the seller's price

So we come to the crunch. You find a house that you believe you want, close to your cash maximum. You know that *everybody* always pays more for their house than they intended, but this need not mean paying the seller's asking price.

There is no exact science in pricing a house and the asking price sometimes bears little relation to its market value. *A house is only worth what somebody will pay for it, and before a house is put up for sale, nobody knows what somebody else will pay.*

The seller may fix on a price that he 'needs', i.e. a price that covers his next house purchase. But that is his problem – you're not buying his next house for him! The seller may fix on a price after having had the house valued by a professional, but where do these professionals get their valuations from? What they think similar houses are selling for in the district, or what they think people might pay for it in current market conditions? The seller's asking price is just a price that the guy is looking for; it may be the maximum he hopes to get, or the minimum he will accept.

Some people will sell a house at any reasonable price, as long as they sell it in a hurry:

- Perhaps they are a newly divorced couple, and they intend to sell, divide the pickings and escape.
- Perhaps they are going under financially, cannot afford to keep up the payments, and it's a race between agreeing a sale and foreclosure.
- Perhaps they have inherited the property, want to realise its worth and divide the money as quickly as possible, just in case some long-lost cousin turns up with a claim from Australia.
- Perhaps they are emigrating, or moving to another part of the country, and need to sell to a deadline.

Their desperation to sell may not be obvious until you question their reasons for selling and compare their often vague answers (i.e. white lies) with what you observe. In divorces, one partner may be more keen to sell than the other. Are they embarrassed by questions about their future movements? Financial pressures usually provoke insistent reminders of their 'willingness' to consider an early sale date, though they don't always disclose exactly why they need to sell. Sometimes an end-of-the-month date is a give-away, especially if it's imminent. In a recent case, I noted that the seller was also heavily committed in a commercial building project and correctly surmised that he needed a quick sale to fill a financial hole.

Beneficiaries of wills often do not have the same attachment as their parents, or uncles and aunts, had to a property, and their sole interest is in selling it quickly. They are unfussy about the price and often take a low offer just to get their hands on the cash. Look for evidence that the late departed owners lived alone, that the sellers are from out of town and/or that the house is in poor decorative order. A hint that all the furniture and fittings are going to the saleroom suggests that the sellers are uninterested in the outcome. It is also helpful when the vultures fall out among themselves over the division of the loot. Bad-tempered inheritance fights are good news for buyers – the sellers screw each other out of spite.

Always ask the seller how long the property has been on the market. It might have been for sale since last spring. If the seller hesitates, or the agent camouflages his answer ('*We've* been handling this for only a week,' meaning that somebody else has been trying to sell it for six months!), perhaps they're treating you to good old evasion. You need to know how long a house has been on the market – after all, you're thinking of going into debt to buy the property. What's more, Superdealers know about the direct connection between the length of time a house has been on the market and the realism of the price that is being asked for it.

There is *One Great Law of the House Market* that is taught in every estate agency in the world: *if the price is too high people won't buy*. It has its corollary: *if people ain't buying, it's because the price is too high*. It follows then that, if a house has been on the market for more than a month, their asking price is too high! When you discover sellers in this situation, you can let them know, gently but firmly, that you want them to share with you an appreciation of the *One Great Law of the House Market*.

This does not mean, of course, that owners will necessarily adjust their price expectations to a realistic level when they are confronted by the brute facts of experience. Irrational hopes drive people to absurd prices in the marketplace, and this is especially true with houses.

It's also a fact of life that prolonged delays in selling a house weary all but the most psychopathic of sellers. If a house doesn't sell, the owners privately feel a mixture of guilt and anger at the implied rejection by the world of the charms of their *El Magnifico*. This causes stress in the household concerned – one partner blames the other for the price, the timing, the conditions, the way they show people round, what they did or didn't do about a half-hearted/promising enquiry and so on. Anybody viewing the house can sense when the sellers are fed up with the whole business. Their scripted lines about the property's features have lost their sparkle and are said with a dullness of wit common to second-rate actors engaged in Take 27 ('This time, Harry, *please*, with *feeling*').

Some people like to 'chat-up' owners, to 'sound them out' about price and perhaps inclusive extras (the furniture, the carpets and fittings, etc.), but this can muddle the deal. Informal chats with sellers can be confusing when one partner tells you one thing (a 'come on') and the other claims ignorance of the concession: 'He couldn't have offered you the clothes dryer as it belongs to my mother and she wants it back.' Agents also have a habit of disclaiming responsibility for concessions made informally: 'You'd best sort that out with the owners; our concern is with the house price, not the fittings.'

This is not to say that you should ignore what the sellers have to say, whether they say it separately or together. Compare notes with your partner on any conversations you have, especially if these give you clues as to the owners' circumstances ('she said they have to move house within three weeks'; 'he's keen to sell as much furniture as possible to save removal costs'; 'she said they'd had an offer but the guy had backed out only yesterday and that they were terribly disappointed').

For Superdealers, all these clues can prove to be useful bargaining leverage. The sellers are probably negotiating privately with themselves ('our price is too damn high,' says one to the other in the quietness of their misery) and they are emotionally ready for a sale.

Of course, if you ignore this possibility, by assuming that *El Dumpo* is hot when it is ice cold, you cannot complain if the seller takes you for the chump that you are. If you do want to buy the house, tell them that it isn't selling because the price is too high, and you happen to be ready to offer a more realistic price if they are ready to sell.

Making an offer

The only offer that counts is the formal offer, in writing, stating your terms and your conditions, with a time limit on them accepting. It should include:

(1) The price you will pay (in England, always 'subject to contract').
There is no reason, other than your own assessment of the competition, why your opening offer should be the same or greater than the seller's opening price, but *beware*: sellers always exaggerate the extent of the competition (so do most buyers when their imagination joins with their emotions about how badly they want the house in question). The seller may operate on the 'bird in hand' philosophy, however, and therefore believe that your firm offer beats vague expressions of interest from other potential buyers.

(2) The inclusions that you require (fittings, carpets, curtains, fixtures, furniture, etc.).
Here you should give yourself lots of negotiating room: include *everything* you can think of, not forgetting the garden hose and tools, and special features you like, especially any the owners might take with them. A friend bought a Georgian flat in Edinburgh New Town and was shocked to find, on entry day, that the previous owners had replaced the Adam fireplaces with modern tiled jobs and all the original brasswork with perspex and plastic! The owners may agree to your requirements, or they may demur; requirements are always negotiable but only if you include them to start with.

This clause in your written offer also has the advantage that a failure of the seller to agree on *any* single item you list gives you a legal right to back out if you change your mind in the meantime.

(3) The conditions that must be met (what you require them to do to make the house habitable, such as paint the windows, fix anything that's broken, etc.).
There are bound to be defects in any property requiring you to put them right at your own expense unless you sensibly require the sellers to do so at theirs.

Again the owners may demur but they may not. This is to your advantage, and anyway it has the additional benefit that it puts pressure on the sellers' inclinations to defend their opening price and to expect more for *El Dumpo*. Obvious things that need putting right justify your lower offer price.

(4) The preferred entry date (chosen to suit you).
Entry dates do not always suit both parties. They may want you to complete the deal earlier because they have bought another house, or later because they need time to find another house. An early entry date might persuade the sellers to accept a lower price if an early sale is in their interest; likewise, a later entry date if the circumstances are different.

Do not leave it open by using an 'entry subject to mutual agreement' clause, as this can lock you into a commitment contrary to your future interests. If they require a shorter/longer amount of time, you can trade off for a profitable adjustment elsewhere in your offer.

(5) The closing date of the offer, after which time it is cancelled unless accepted by the sellers, but reserving your right to cancel the offer at any time before the closing date.
Never make offers that are open for an indefinite term. They can sit on your offer while they see if they can persuade another buyer to do better. Remember the possibilities of gazumping – a time deadline on your offer won't save you from being gazumped but it does limit the amount of time you are at risk of a Dutch auction.

The time that an offer is valid can be very short (I've put in an offer at 2 pm valid until 5 pm that same day) or relatively longer, say, several days (*never* more than a week!) to allow an absentee owner to be contacted.

The purpose of the deadline is to concentrate the sellers' minds on your offer, which may or may not be what they hoped to get, and on the fact that your certain offer will lapse on a specific date. The statement that you may withdraw your offer at *any time* before it formally lapses puts even more pressure on the sellers because they do not know whether you might be withdrawing your offer at the very moment that they are dithering about what to do.

(6) The 'lifeboat' clause.

A 'lifeboat clause' is one that gives you a get out if something goes wrong, or you discover things that you did not suspect when you made your offer. You may not have to use your lifeboat clause, but at sea and in the house market, when you need a lifeboat, *you need a lifeboat*! An example of one of these is:

This offer is contingent on the veracity of all statements made by the seller in respect of the property, including its structural soundness and condition, and approval by the buyer of all encumbrances and planning changes that might affect the property, whether presently known or not, and any other material facts that may affect the buyer's interests.

If you can get away with this – and particularly the words 'and approval by the buyer of . . . any other material facts that may affect the buyer's interests' – you are safe because it gives you almost unlimited licence to jump into the lifeboat if circumstances suggest it is in your interests to do so.

Do you need an estate agent?

Handing the sale of your house over to an estate agent and then taking a back seat is as shortsighted as trying to sell it yourself without considering what is involved.

Estate agents, and solicitors, are no different from any other group of professionals. Most are good, a few are very good and a minority are bloody awful. No profession is free from fools, and in choosing an agent you could get stuck with that profession's version of Inspector Clouseau. You might even be unfortunate enough to sign up with somebody who is normally very good, only to find that they are going through a bad patch: he or she is in love, needs a holiday, has their mind on something else, or they are too busy to spare the time to do a good job on this occasion.

Estate agents live by selling property on behalf of clients, but this does not mean that they are as diligent in respect of every client. If they don't sell your house, but manage to sell some others, they are doing well by their standards.

Much of what an estate agent does can be done by anyone, and you must decide whether you wish, or are able, to undertake the agency tasks yourself. Many people successfully sell their own homes and save the agent's fee (between 1 and 3 per cent of the gross selling price, plus all advertising costs). You can judge for yourself whether to use an agent by considering the mechanics of selling a house, summarised in the next few pages. But remember, whether you do or do not use an agent, you will still have to do a lot of the work yourself if you are to get the best price.

Agents advise on the price you should put on your house

An agent's advice is based on the prices that are being asked for similar houses in similar locations, given the state of the market and so on. The agent's price can be above or below the actual market price the house eventually realises, which is *only* what somebody is willing to pay for it. If hordes of people view it, you know you are close to being right; if nobody turns up, you know you are closer to being wrong.

You can get an idea of your property's worth by comparing the prices of similar houses advertised in local newspapers and in the display windows of local estate agents, or by paying for a valuation from a surveyor.

You can (cheeky!) ask an estate agent for a free valuation and then not use their services. Some agents block off this ploy by waiving valuation fees only if they become your agent.

Agents prepare advertising and place it in suitable media, including their own windows

All expenses of advertising are charged to you, and deducted at source from the buyer's cheque or, in the event of a 'no-sale', are invoiced to you direct – the 'no sale, no fee' promise offered by many agents refers only to the selling fee they charge if the house is sold, and this fee excludes the cost of advertising.

Estate agents, advertising in papers, always use large type for their own name and address, and sometimes display a logo as well. This takes up half (or more!) of the advertisement space that you are paying for, and is a free advert for themselves. Instead, you can prepare your own advertising and use all the space you pay for solely to advertise your house. Similarly, the 'FOR SALE' sign outside your house need only include a phone number, instead of being another free advertisement for the estate agent.

Agents prepare a list of particulars about your house to circulate to potential buyers

It's almost certain that you will have to provide most of this information yourself, or at least confirm it, for nobody knows a house better than those who live in it.

Agents might measure the room sizes for you, and this could be the only time they visit the house they are selling. You can, of course, measure the rooms yourself and enter the details in your own printed particulars, including a sentence stating that the 'particulars are for information only and do not constitute a legal contract'. It is up to the buyer to verify all your statements.

In many cases, you will have to walk viewers round the house yourself. As agents sell dozens of houses at a time, and they need to be in their offices too, and seldom work evenings, except for higher fees, it restricts viewing times if they are in charge of the viewing sessions.

There is no reason why you can't prepare your particulars yourself, and get it printed at a local printing shop or secretarial agency (and photocopy copies as you need them).

Agents receive offers from buyers and bring them to your attention

Those offers that are satisfactory are likely to be obvious to you. What you do about an unsatisfactory offer (is it a buyer's try-on? is your asking price that far out? should you hang on for a better offer? can you push the offer up?) is up to you, and you may get precious little useful advice from agents: 'Ring me back when you have made up your mind,' might be the only help you get.

Some agents, of course, will protest and say that this is a libel on their profession, and it is true that most agents *some* of the time do help their clients with these decisions, but it is the rest of the time that counts, and you may well be left to make such decisions on your own.

You will be more interested in a specific decision to accept or reject a disappointing offer than agents will be, because if you decide to accept, they know they have 'earned' a fee (about 3 per cent of the sale price), and if you try for a better offer, they are not risking anything as all advertising and other costs are charged to you anyway, plus there is the prospect of a larger fee from a bigger price.

If you decide to accept an offer, the agent hands over the next steps in the process to your solicitor. Conveyancing, or the passing of legal title from a seller to a buyer, is handled by solicitors, though again you can do most of this yourself.

In summary, agents will help to sell your house. They do this for a living and should be more competent at it than somebody doing it for the first time, though this need not be the case. However, much of what the average agent does, you are perfectly capable of doing yourself, and given what you have to do to prepare and conduct the sale whether you use an agent or not, you may conclude that an agent is somebody who gets 3 per cent for doing what you must do for yourself anyway. And doing your sums you might be shocked to find that using an agent to 'help' you to sell your house for £83,000 costs you about £2490 in fees, plus several hundred pounds more in sharing advertisements with his business, plus the conveyancing costs, plus any stamp duty the government takes from you!

Since there is more competition now in the house-selling business, some agents are actively touting for business. You should be ready to deal with such approaches, not all of which are in your best interests to encourage.

Like any other business, agents scan the market for leads. Some come from friends who hear of a colleague at work, or a neighbour, about to sell their house, or experiencing difficulty in selling one already. Other leads come from watching the local papers to see who is selling on their own or which competing agents have houses that are stuck. On the basis of these leads, they make an approach. They are not worried about cutting in on another agent's arrangement with you, nor are they backward when trying to crash into your effort to sell without an agent. However, as a seller, you have distinct interests, and there is no need to jeopardise these when you get a call from an estate agent, apparently anxious to help you sell your house.

The agent's pitch might go along the following lines:

I think I might be able to sell your house quickly for you. For the usual fee, I'll view your house, bring along my client, Mr Ahmed, and we might be able to agree a purchase in a couple of days.

You should immediately note that this agent is in an ambiguous position. Just who is he representing: you or his 'client'?

Clarify this by asking him directly: waffle indicates that he is working both of you against each other for a larger fee. Another pertinent question is: does he have a 'client' or is it a ploy to become your agent? Is he going to lead you along and then drop the news that 'Unfortunately, Mr Ahmed decided to buy another house, but I will get a new buyer for you'?

Providing you have not previously agreed to anything, you can decline his services when he does the 'client has bolted' ploy. However, you may already have become a victim of a con. For a clue as to his real intentions, watch his demeanour when he comes to view your house on behalf of his alleged client, and see if he tries to get you to sign an agency agreement with him. He might claim: 'It is a "perfect match" with Mr Ahmed's requirements, *so if you will sign this agency agreement,* I will bring him round on Thursday morning.' Once you sign the agreement (a 'gotcha' if ever there was one), he then springs on you, a day or so later, the 'client has bolted' ploy ('Mr Ahmed has bought something else'). If you sign an exclusive house-selling agreement, you are legally obligated to pay his fee if the house is sold, even if it is exclusively as a result of your own efforts, or another agent's!

Alternatively, he might play the 'switch sale' ploy with:

It's not quite what Mr Ahmed is looking for, but I get people in the office every week looking for houses like this – I sold one just like it last week and got £2000 more than you are asking – *so if you sign this agency agreement,* I'll find you a buyer right away.

You should never sign anything under these circumstances.

If you want an agent, fine, but if you aren't careful, one can creep into the sale on false pretences – your gullibility that a sale is imminent – and you will be legally required to pay the agent's fee no matter who sells the house. And remember that this obligation to pay a commission on the sale applies to any agent who is already commissioned to sell your house: they all get a dip into the honey pot (i.e. your income from the sale), no matter how many agents you commission.

If, however, you are tempted to test the agent's truthfulness (after all, there may be a genuine client just waiting to bid for your house), you can do three things:

1. *Require him to acknowledge* in writing **that he is** not **acting as your agent, nor may he advertise or enter into any expenses on**

your behalf. He must state that he is solely acting as Mr Ahmed's agent (insist on a named 'client', as an absence of a name is suspicious and might commit you to an agency commission).
This written confirmation prevents him extending his grip on your house sale beyond a phoney introduction.

2. You only agree to pay an 'introduction to Mr Ahmed' fee if, and only if, Mr Ahmed buys your house as a result of the agent's introduction. If Mr Ahmed backs out of the deal, then you have no agency agreement with the agent.
The 'introduction to Mr Ahmed' fee (nowhere acknowledged as an agency fee) must be less than the 3 per cent an agent normally charges for his services. As the agent claims to have a client available now, he will not need to undertake any of these agency services. Tell him that he will get a percentage from your house sale only if Mr Ahmed buys, which is good money for doing very little; otherwise, he doesn't.

3. Do not sign anything he hands you that can be remotely interpreted as commissioning him to find you a seller. He might try to bluff you that all estate agents work from 'standard forms', etc. Tell him that, if he wants to earn his money, he is wasting a lot of time arguing with you about trivia. Write out your terms as above and invite him to sign it.
In the meantime, if you find another buyer, proceed with the sale, secure in the knowledge that, as your efforts sold the house, you need not pay the agent who offered to introduce another purchaser, the mysterious Mr Ahmed.

Suppose, however, a Mr Ahmed does turn up and you do business with him? Simple: pay the agent the introductory fee when the sale is completed (never pay a penny on the basis of Mr Ahmed's offer, for offers, like agents' 'introductions', have a shorter life than a butterfly). If the agent has done his job, he is worth his fee – though push him on the amount!

Dealing with price pressure from buyers

As a seller, you are interested in the *total price* the house realises. This need not be the case with the buyer. Why? Because most buyers do not buy a house with cash out of their own pocket. Normally, they borrow all, or most, of the purchase price, using their savings or the equity they realised from their previous house to cover what they cannot borrow.

Buyers have a vague idea of the total price they can afford to pay, which firms up when they sell their own house. You should attempt to find out the specific circumstances relating to each potential buyer:

- How they are financing the purchase. Cash? Savings plus a mortgage? With or without a house to sell?
- How much they expect to get for their house.

A *cash purchaser* has certain attractions to a seller (no danger of a mortgage problem); on the other hand, people with cash concentrate on the total price and you may get more than normal pressure from them to do an *El Cheapo*. Cash buyers often think they are the most valuable of customers to the seller. Disabuse them of this by pretending it makes no difference to you who buys the house or how they finance the purchase, as you are in no hurry at all. Whoever gives you the best price gets the house; otherwise they don't.

In contrast, *buyers with savings and a mortgage* are often vulnerable to the 'bagatelle', which plays on the thinness of the slices they have to pay each month rather than the total price of the house. Mortgages are paid monthly, and for many people it is the monthly payment that counts, not the total price. Such people tend to buy a house if they can afford to pay the monthly payment, and they are less careful about the total price.

Buyers with houses to sell need not discourage you: many thousands of houses sell each month, recessions notwithstanding. You are interested in the equity the buyers hope to make from selling their own houses, for this enables you to try the 'cheap at half the price' ploy.

Buyers who have a house already think about how much they have available to purchase their next house (hopefully yours!). The amount of their equity is an important consideration in the buying of your house. Consider a simple arithmetical example: Assume that you paid £20,000 for a house in 1980. Of that £20,000, you borrowed, say, £15,000 from a building society or bank in the form of a standard repayment mortgage. Therefore, your initial equity in the house at the time of your purchase was £5000. Now, if you sell the house in 1988 for £60,000, and owe by then, say, £11,000 on your 1980 mortgage, and your selling costs are £3000, your owner's equity can be calculated as follows: £60,000 minus £11,000 = £49,000; deduct selling costs of £3000 = £46,000. This is your equity.

Your equity has grown from £5000 in 1980 to about £46,000 in 1988. Part of the growth in equity comes from the reduction in your mortgage burden from £15,000 to £11,000, but by far the largest part is due to the appreciation in the money value of the house from £20,000 to £60,000.

How then does the 'cheap at half the price' ploy work? Largely by playing on the equity illusion of the buyer.

Suppose that they have, or expect to have, £46,000 in equity available from their current house, and suppose that you are selling yours for £85,000. The buyers have to find £85,000 less £46,000, or £39,000, perhaps from a building society or a bank, and this figure is, plausibly, the 'price' of your house to them. You can bet that £39,000 will be the figure that they concentrate on in their private debates about whether to buy your house or not. If they can borrow £39,000, they can buy your house, and will put less pressure on your price than if they can't.

It is likely that £39,000 is on the margin of their borrowing limit because most buyers tend to go close to their limits in house purchase. In this case, draw attention to prospects of a rapid price appreciation of your house ('it's doubled in value since we moved in three years ago'). This supports the positive reasons they might have for buying your house. In effect, you tell them that they can acquire your £85,000 house for less than half its total price, i.e. £39,000. Far from being expensive, it's actually cheap – 'a sound family investment', etc. – because the real price they are paying, which is the amount that they have to borrow, is less than half the price that the house is worth. Psychologically, the buyers can be geared up to think (if they are not already doing so!) in terms of paying £39,000 for your house and not £85,000.

Why?

Human nature! They believe that their £46,000 equity stake is 'free' because they get it from the buyer of their own house. It's the £39,000 that they borrow for the next twenty years that costs them money, and it is this amount that they consider when they have the opportunity to acquire a house worth more than twice as much.

By understanding how average buyers see their own financial situation, you can see why the pressure is not on you and your price. You do not have to negotiate with yourself and cut your price because the buyer considers the £39,000 loan and not the £85,000 price.

Does this sound far-fetched? Are you sceptical that people go for such an obvious ploy? You would be wrong!

Great efforts are made in sales training to get sellers to refrain from mentioning the total cost of whatever it is that they are selling and to concentrate the buyer's attention instead on the (much smaller) monthly, daily or hourly cost. The point is: as these techniques work in business, they can be made to work for you.

How to sell *El Magnifico*

Why *El Magnifico*? Because if you don't see your house in the best light, you might come to believe that you live in *El Dumpo*.

Prepare the house well, present it properly, make it easy for the buyer to come to a 'yes' decision, and you'll be counting your cash before your neighbours know you've gone.

To prepare your house for sale, take a good look at it, inside and outside. Walk up to it from along the street and examine its flaws. Everything you see (and a few things you miss) will be seen critically by your viewers (in houses, as in spouses, there's no accounting for taste!).

Is there anything you can do to improve its appearance at low cost? Yes, lots.

- A new coat of paint on the window frames, the door, and the gate.
- Does the gate open easily? If not, why not?
- Fix broken or cracked windows and wash them.
- Is the front garden like a rubbish tip?
- Cut the hedge, mow the lawn, weed the flowerbeds, tidy up any shrubs and trees.
- Hire a skip and remove all rubbish.

'RISING DAMP? NO, I CAN'T SAY I'VE NOTICED ANY.'

- Check out the taps, toilets, door handles, window latches, light switches, floorboards, central heating, etc.
- Clean the rooms.
- Place flowers and potted plants about the property.
- N.B. *Houses that smell seldom sell!*

Having done all this – and it is hard work – your house will be more presentable as *El Magnifico*.

All buyers may be thieves, but you want to do business with them. Why? Because if you don't get a buyer, you can't sell your house.

The buyers, therefore, are not your enemy. They can be of

great benefit to you, providing you get them to make you an offer; otherwise, it's been a great waste of time (except for the experience).

First, stop talking about your *house* – you are selling your *home*, and homes like motherhood and apple pie are 'feel goods' (you 'feel good' when you visualise them). Make it less impersonal. Estate agents sell houses not homes, so give yourself the edge.

Second, when showing buyers around refer to '*your* sitting-room', '*your* bedroom', '*your* garden' and so on. Why? Professionals call this the *assumptive close* – you are assuming they are going to buy, which induces feelings of ownership and gives the green light to their urge to buy.

Third, show them the property properly by leading them round the rooms. Don't step aside at the door and leave them to timidly enter a strange space. If you stop near the door, they will too. Get into the room and, by your entry, draw them right into it too.

Fourth, start off in the best room, conduct them round the property and bring them back to the best room (you can start and end in the garden if it's a lovely garden *and* a lovely day).

Fifth, keep the family and the pets out of the way during viewing hours. Barking dogs and nervous cats are a distraction (animals are not odourless either). Children and irascible grannies and grandads can get between you and a sale, especially if the viewers have the 'cheek' to interrupt favourite soap operas and TV quizzes.

Sixth, have cleanly printed particulars available for each viewer, preferably with a photo of the house. Get your local fast photo shop to do up 25 copies of a print taken by an ordinary camera – it's well worth the investment as a selling expense.

Seventh, make yourself available to discuss the property and the nature of the deal they might make with you. Specify your availability for informal discussions outside the viewing time, with your daytime and home phone numbers on the particulars sheet.

Handling the buyer's crunch questions

Sellers and buyers do not have perfect information about each other's intentions. You don't know the highest price the buyer might pay for *El Magnifico*; the buyer doesn't know the lowest price you will accept for *El Dumpo*.

Neither of you knows what's in the other's mind. You glean information by asking questions and listening to the answers. Answers and volunteered statements either help a sale or they don't. Anything that helps a sale is a green light for the buyer to proceed; anything that hinders the sale flashes a red warning light for them to be cautious. Your aim is to give more green lights than red ones.

An obvious opening question from the buyer is: *'Why are you selling this house?'*

Your answer gives clues to any pressure on you to sell. If you tell them, for example:

My wife has been appointed to a Registrar's post in Sheffield and we must move with the job.

I'm doing a two-year tour in Saudi with my company and we leave in three weeks.

these answers signal that you are eager to sell, perhaps at a lower price because you face a deadline. Buyers put pressure on sellers with deadlines.

Block off pressure by saying:

We are moving to another location following a promotion, and all selling and removal expenses, including (thank God!) any bridging finance, are being paid by the employer. Therefore we can wait to get our asking price.

A variation on the 'why are you selling?' question is the disarmingly simple one: *'How long has this house been on the market?'* Whatever you do, don't confess to the house being stuck. Think about your answer *before* you face the question, otherwise you enhance the buyer's leverage. A fumbled answer signals 'squeeze my price'!

A stuck house also worries a buyer: is it falling down, or is there an amenity defect they don't know about (planned motorway, airport, prison, council estate), or subsidence, asbestos tip, etc. Ignorance may be bliss, but there is nothing quite as offputting, in both houses and *affaires de coeur*, as a gnawing suspicion that something is not quite kosher.

Suppose you are having difficulty selling your house: need it be a knock-out defeat for your sale?

No! Rise to the Superdeal role; after all, you are in the theatre of negotiation, except there is no agreed script!

Tell them, for example:

I put the house on the market earlier in the year because I thought I was being transferred to the Bolton office, but [shrugging your shoulders] head office changed their mind – once again! – and postponed my transfer, forcing me to take it off the market. We lost a keen buyer who couldn't wait, and it was all quite embarrassing. Now, instead of a mere transfer, I've now been promoted, but not (fortunately) to Bolton.

Will they believe you? Perhaps! If they do, they will refrain from a major push on your price. They certainly won't if you lamely confess: 'Yes, our house is stuck.'

Use your imagination to fit your circumstances. For example, an Oscar-winning performance might go something like:

We thought we were going to have a baby but [dropping your voice to a whisper] we lost it and we had to take the house off the market for a while. [A woman could buy that as an explanation, but wives should expect implicit sympathy as the viewers leave!]

A house new on the market still prompts the question: *'Why are you selling it?'* A credible answer enhances the merits of the house (a green light); a poor one flashes a red light. For example, 'We need another room because of the new baby' floats the thought that a house too small for you is also too small for them. Avoid references to your need for additional space. Try to find out the buyer's needs as you take them round the house. Ask questions like:

- 'What kind of house are you looking for?'
- 'Do you have any children?'
- 'Is the house for yourselves?'

If they are bringing hordes of kids with them, emphasise what a wonderful house it is for children (roomy, safe and lots of neighbours with kids). If they don't have children and want peace and quiet, tell them how ideal it is for retirement (compact, easy to manage, quiet neighbours). If they are buying it for their son and his family, tell them what a good investment it is and how you made a lovely family home, and so on.

Indicating problems with neighbours, or problems with any-thing related to the locality, are red-light answers: 'We like the town but can't stand the neighbours' or 'I find the traffic just too much' are candid but hardly increase your chances of a sale. People avoid bad neighbours, and they don't go a bundle on traffic jams.

In fact, the less said about your neighbours the better, and anything that is said should be of a complimentary nature, or better still: 'They keep themselves pretty much to themselves.' Nothing should ever be said about traffic.

It is essential, therefore, to rehearse the reasons for your moving before the viewers turn up. Consider the impact of any information on the buyer, not the veracity of the information itself – you are not under oath. Your story need not be untrue (heaven forbid!), but it should be at least vaguely credible. There is only one thing worse than having an unbelievable story – that is having more than one story told to viewers depending on which of you shows them round. Buyers (rightly!) sometimes send friends round for an opinion. They compare notes and discrepancies in your tales, sometimes exposing your real motives for moving.

Another obvious (though not always asked) question is: *'What's wrong with the house structurally?'*

This can be difficult to handle. You are not obliged to draw their attention to defects but you might be legally liable if you deliberately lie about any that you are aware of. Problems can arise if defects come to light only after you leave (can you prove you were unaware of them?). You can say, if there was a problem: 'Three years ago, the roof was damaged in a storm, but this was repaired by Roofeasy Fixers Ltd. Their survey and the work they did, plus the insurance company's payment, can be seen in these photocopies, which you may keep.'

The 'killer' question you must be ready to answer is: *'What price are you* really *looking for?'* Is this a speculative try-on aimed at an instant price cut – which would immediately follow if you said you would take anything less than your quoted price – or a genuine opening of a negotiation by a serious buyer wanting to do business?

Tell them: 'I'm looking for the best price I can get. What do you have in mind?' This puts the onus on them to propose something. Your price is on the table, the buyer can respond. If you move first, it will lead to one-way movement by you, not the buyer.

If they say your house is 'too expensive', it may well be true, both in the sense that it is too expensive for them (above their cash maximum), or for everybody (you've over-priced it). You can't do anything about the former – you're not their bank manager – and it may be too soon to do anything about the latter – you have not tested the market for long enough.

It is up to buyers to make you an offer, not for you to auction your property downwards until a buyer says 'yes'. Concede nothing in a question session. Shuffle them towards an offer.

Your objective is to lead buyers to make you an offer, preferably in writing. Such offers should include:

- The price they are offering to pay for the title to the property itself.
- What, if anything, they want included in the sale (fittings, carpets, fixtures, furniture, etc.).
- Any relevant conditions they want met (repairs, replacement features such as putting the garage doors back on their hinges, etc.).
- Their suggested completion date.

You need not agree to any or all of the details of a written offer. *You certainly won't agree to any 'lifeboat' clauses!* And be careful about any pre-emptive dates for acceptance of the offer, unless, of course, an immediate sale on their terms suits you.

What is and is not acceptable to you is subject to negotiation.

The 'surveyor's lament' and its counters

A basic principle in the opening stages of any negotiation is to avoid committing yourself to anything. You only respond in specific terms to a specific (preferably written) offer. True, you can signal the possibility of flexibility but only by the deftest of language:

Buyer: Are the carpets and curtains [or anything else] included?
Seller: Some of them might be if the total offer matched our expectations.

Buyer: What sort of completion date are you looking for?
Seller: That would depend on the offer. For the right price, we would consider a mutually convenient completion date.

The 'surveyor's lament' is one ploy that you must be ready for. This is usually introduced in the following way:

Buyer: If we were to make an offer, would you take the house off the market?
Seller: If the offer and completion date were good enough, we could consider that.

Whether the house is off or on the market while the necessary house sale formalities are being sorted out can become very important as the negotiations progress, for once it is taken off the market on receipt of an offer, and a deposit, you are vulnerable to the 'surveyor's lament':

Since the house was surveyed, we must reduce our offer to take account of the £4000-worth of work that needs to be done.

or:

The surveyor's valuation scuppered our chances of getting the mortgage we expected and we must reduce our offer by £2000.

Either way, you are in a weak position. Say 'no' and it is costly and time-consuming to put your house on the market again; say 'yes' and you get less for your house.

Your choice depends on your leverage. If you are forced to say 'yes' but you had an inclusive deal with the buyers – carpets, fittings, fixtures and so on – you can undo some of the damage by undoing that part of the deal: 'If you change the price, I must take out the fixtures and fittings.' Be firm on this, as a deal is a deal until it's no longer a deal!

Try, also, to resist their drop in price by saying you will only come down, say, £500 in view of the circumstances *but no more*. For a drop in price greater than £500, the house goes on the market again.

The best way to prevent being caught with a surveyor's lament is to require an *option* instead of a deposit:

Buyer: If we were to make an offer, would you take the house off the market?
Seller: That would depend on the offer, and if that is satisfactory to me, I would be prepared, for £500, to assign you an exclusive option to buy the property at the agreed price for a period of eight weeks.

This won't be appropriate in all cases, particularly in a buyer's market, but it can be used on good-quality property, and even on very ordinary property an option can be negotiated that is not too onerous on the buyer. Options are widely used in business, particularly in property transactions, and they are perfectly legal if the parties agree to one.

Most estate agents require buyers to put up a small deposit as a sign of their seriousness, and for many years, a sum of £100 was the regularly recognised deposit. In practice, it is returnable if the sale falls through, such as if a buyer's chain breaks. With an option, the rules are different. The buyer pays you a sum of money for an *exclusive* option on the property for an agreed price. If he buys the property within the option period (eight, ten, twelve weeks), his option can be part of his payment; if, for any reason, he does not buy the property, you pocket the option fee.

Now option fees are not a way of ripping off buyers (in fact, they are sound insurance for them), nor should the terms be so onerous that they lose their money if new circumstances arise that were unforeseen by both parties. However, options do give you leverage against buyers if they try a surveyor's lament.

Set the option at £500 and you will have something to finance a return to the market. Buyers know this and are therefore unlikely to try it on. You negotiate with them from a stronger position.

Why should buyers agree to options and not deposits? Because if they have an option, you cannot gazump them as they have an exclusive right to buy your house for an agreed sum for the period of the option. That is a benefit to them and they might consider it worthwhile, especially in a sellers' market.

Don't concede – trade!

Negotiations between seller and buyer are the final act in their relationship. Agree on a price and its associated conditions and the deal is done; fail to agree and each has to search for another deal with someone else. Let's walk through some negotiating scenarios and pick out the essential message of *Superdeal*: never concede – trade instead!

You might think that you want the other guy to say 'yes' to your first offer. Well, you are entirely wrong, and if you think more carefully about it, you should see why.

Consider his interpretation of your 'yes' to his offer: surely you are telling the buyer that his offer is good enough for you, whatever it is for him, and, in fact, it's so good for you that you do not hesitate to say 'yes' to it! What does that mean to him? Surely, that he has got it wrong: there may be a better offer (for him) – a lower price, less onerous terms, more side concessions from you, etc. – that would suit him better. Of course, this may not be true. His offer may just have been enough for you to say 'yes' but no more. However, he does not know this, and not knowing causes doubts about the deal.

Negotiation consists of people making opening offers that are best for themselves, and then moving towards each other until they find an offer that is good enough for both of them. You know that the opening offer is not where you expect to end up whatever you aver to the contrary. You expect to have to move, hopefully in return for the other guy moving.

For example, the buyer's opening offer is the best offer for him – after all, he chose it! Logically, if he moves on his opening offer, it must make his offer better for you than his opening one. Hence, by definition, his opening offer is the 'worst' for you, and it can be improved upon.

From the other point of view, when the buyer constructs his opening offer, he knows that you may want him to improve on it. Therefore, it follows that you know that he knows his opening offer is not yet his best offer (for you)!

Consequently, do not say 'yes' to an opening offer, no matter how good it appears to be at first glance. Try to improve on it. However, to flatly reject a 'good' offer would be foolhardy, although you can reject a *totally* inadequate one. Tell him that his offer is interesting but that it is not yet good enough. However, merely saying 'no' won't improve his offer and might lead him to look elsewhere for a more informative negotiator, so you should also tell him what he has to do to improve it. This may mean more money if you're selling, less if you're buying, or different sets of inclusions and conditions. Specify how you want these altered. This tells him that you mean business and how he can do business with you.

If your asking price was a straight £82,000, watch out for an offer price of £78,000. What price is being hinted at here? Why, £80,000 of course. Similarly, an offer of £45,000 against an asking price of £50,000 suggests £47,500. To avoid this, put your price in odd numbers (£82,750 or £44,800, for example) and beyond 'split the difference' arithmetic.

Any move you make on your price must be 'paid for' by concessions from the other guy. The alternative risks disaster:

Seller: I couldn't take less than £50,000.
Buyer: My absolute best is £49,000.
Seller: You must get to £50,000 or it's no deal.
Buyer: No way. Its £49,250 or no deal.
Seller: Make it £50,000 and we have a deal.
Buyer: OK, agreed.

What happened? The buyer certainly moved up, from £49,000 to £50,000, while the seller stood still at £50,000. This may or may not be within your cash maximum, but you moved and he didn't. In fact, the buyer's behaviour rewarded the seller for standing still: every 'no' brought forth a price concession, teaching the seller to say 'no' and see what he gets for doing so.

Suppose, however, that the buyer's demands went way beyond price and included such things as the furniture, furnishings and fittings of the house. Could he protect his position, and get a deal, by unilateral conceding? I doubt it.

The Superdeal way to negotiate is to trade one thing for another. This way you get something back for your concessions to the buyer:

Buyer: I'll offer you £48,500.
Seller: I couldn't take less than £50,000.
Buyer: If you include the carpets and the curtains I'll go to £48,750.
Seller: If you reach £49,900 I'll include the upstairs fitted carpets.
Buyer: Include all the carpets, and I'll go to £48,900.
Seller: I'll include all the fitted carpets if you agree to £49,750 but you must complete in thirty days.
Buyer: For £49,000 I would require the fitted carpets, and the curtains.
Seller: Providing you put £3000 down, and offer £49,500 I'll agree to the fitted carpets and the curtains, except those in the master bedroom.
Buyer: I'll put £1000 down, and offer £49,250 but you must include the washing machine.
Seller: Make that £49,450 and I'll include the curtains in the master bedroom and leave behind the garden chairs.
Buyer: Agreed.

Each move this time was accompanied by a specific trade from the other party. The illustration's moves and monetary values are not as important as the method: in the real world, the trade-offs will vary in their value to each side.

The main point is that each offered to move to get movement from the other. It was not a one-way auction with one party making all the concessions, nor was the negotiation merely confined to price. The carpets, curtains and garden chairs, for example, could be in any condition from acceptable to appalling. The point is that you trade to get movement from the other guy.

How to let and rent

While the poor rent because they have no choice, most of us rent something at sometime or another because it is convenient to do so. It could be our house while we are abroad, or while we are caught in a bridging trap. It could be a holiday home, a boat and, more commonly, a car (*see* p. 130). Sometimes we are letting and sometimes we are renting.

There are Superdeals to be made on both sides of the transaction.

Letting your property, either temporarily or for the duration, requires that you, or your agent, keeps control of its management. A property deteriorates when the owners neglect to manage it, and the tenants have no incentive to look after it or its contents. Hence, the first rule of letting: *keep control of the property and its contents*, by visiting it, checking the specified contents and having fixed-time leases. If you let because of an absence abroad, or live any distance too great for regular supervision, consider a deal with a property manager. Rates for the latter vary – 10 to 15 per cent of the gross income – and they are negotiable.

The second rule is: *select your tenants carefully*. Avoid students (especially medics, architects and engineers; they drink too much at their wild parties, redesign the interiors and interfere with the appliances, respectively), foreign diplomats, relatives and friends (the latter two are bad payers). Corporate lettings are fairly safe: the company takes responsibility for their employees' behaviour.

The third rule is: *you must have a written contract*, specifying the rent and when it can be raised, the rates, the tenants' responsibilities for utilities, telephone and damage to the (agreed) contents, and you keep the *named* tenants to their obligations without fail. You do not allow them to pass on the letting to friends – if they leave, it reverts to you. Otherwise, you might find them long gone, along with the odd item of furniture that they took a shine to, and the new lot, or their successors, a source of grief.

When renting a property yourself, you want to get the loosest terms you can, and as much responsibility for the contents, including the utilities, pushed back to the owner. 'Fair wear-and-tear' is an important principle, otherwise the owner can charge you for the twenty-year-old collapsing divan, or the torn bit of wallpaper in the lavatory. You don't want to receive unannounced inspection visits and can require that you receive reasonable notice of the owner arriving to check the place over.

Your lease should have options for an extension in it, and your right to vary the people who live with you. You don't want to lose your flat because your husband runs off with a dress designer and you make new live-in arrangements with somebody else. You also might have some friends staying over, or even living in while you are away on holiday or business, and you don't want a reversion clause to be enforced in your absence.

How do you get what you want? *First, you must know what you want. Second, you must formulate your wants as proposals. Third, you must trade off your wants for theirs.*

Your checklist

- If you're buying, you make an offer for an *El Dumpo*; if you're selling, you want a price for an *El Magnifico*.
- Most flaws in a house can be put right at little cost and a lot of elbow grease before a sale – so do it. Flaws can be found by attentive buyers, so look for them and adjust your offer price to suit.
- All buyers are thieves, so hold back any concessions that you have available in order to trade them for a better deal when the buyer presents his first (best for him/worst for you) offer.
- All sellers are liars, so ask questions about why they are selling, how long the house has been on the market, what is included in the price.

- Make an offer:
  - below the asking price.
  - inclusive of furniture, furnishings and fittings.
  - with defects you want put right.
  - with a time limit and with a right to withdraw it beforehand.
  - with a lifeboat clause.
- Negotiate using concessions as trades, not free gifts.
- If the buyer won't budge, search for another one. If the seller won't budge, find another house to buy.

Most houses are on the market for less than a month, which means that there is a new market, with new sellers and buyers, about every month.

6

Buying a car

How long is it since you bought a car? Answer this question before you consider buying another one. Unless you purchase cars for a living, you probably buy at intervals no shorter than every two years and, if you are an average buyer, it's more likely to be around every four years.

Now after you have contemplated the frequency of your car buying, consider Jeremiah Jaws, the person who is going to sell you your next car (he becomes a *Jeremiah* when he estimates the value of your trade-in, and *Jaws* when he prices the new one). What has Jaws been doing since you bought your present car? Indeed, what is he doing right now while you are thinking about buying a new one?

Yes, he's been selling cars every working day since you last saw him, and right this very minute he is probably in mid-stream selling to another buyer. And if it's two in the morning just now, you can bet your old car to a new Mercedes that he's dreaming about selling cars – which is why car salesmen deserve the divorce rate of the jet set!

It's remarkable how many people forget this simple truth: *car sellers practise their selling skills every working day.* During an average month, Jaws meets almost every kind of customer there is; he hears nothing he hasn't heard 1001 times before; and he knows, from long years of lucrative tedium, what to do when you walk into his showroom to look at a car you are not sure (yet) you can afford. True, you might walk in and be attended to by Tiddler, the company's most junior salesman on his first day in the car-selling business, but I wouldn't bank on it. The guy you will get, like Jaws, has twenty years' selling experience, and a breakfast appetite for buyers like you. In short, compared to the seller, no matter how good you think you are (and few people are that good), when it comes to buying cars you start off with a major disadvantage: *you* are out of practice; Jaws is just warming up!

What can you do about this?

First, acknowledge your lack of practice and accept that this is a major weakness on your part. *Second*, enhance your negotiating leverage in some way; otherwise, you're at the mercy of the seller.

Most people do not even think about the disadvantages of being out of practice when the stakes are as high as they are with a car purchase (even if driving the car doesn't kill you, financing it might). By just gliding into the showroom, after only a few cursory glances at used-car ads in the papers, you risk taking the same route as the croissants and coffee Jaws had for breakfast.

How do you acquire negotiating leverage?

There is one certain answer to this question: whatever leverage you do acquire, it is more likely to be acquired *before* rather than *after* entering the showroom. In other words, leverage comes from preparation before the negotiation and *not* improvisation during it.

Why do you want to buy a car?

Before doing anything else, carefully think through why you are in the market for a new car.

There are two kinds of reasons for wanting a new car: reasons of substance and reasons of fancy. The first kind give you leverage (because sound reasons are a credible and defendable objective); the latter kind concede it. It's not that I'm against fancy notions as such; it's just that they almost always lead you to pay over the odds for things you want, unless, that is, you have some substantive reasons as well.

Decide into what category your reasons fall by considering some (non-exhaustive) examples of both:

REASONS FOR WANTING A NEW CAR

Facts	Fancy
My current car: won't start	I've just passed my driving test/got my licence back

Facts	Fancy
won't go	Exotic/erotic advertising
is too small/large	I want to impress somebody
is uncomfortable	Self-esteem
has been stolen/smashed	My current car looks scruffy/dated
High and regular repair bills	It's time for a change
	I can afford one
	I'm seeking peer group approval

Reasons of substance – that is, reasons related to facts – give you specific objectives and make Jaws' sales patter sound phoney. Reasons of fancy, however real for you, relate to emotions not to facts and are the mirror-image of sales patter, much beloved by the creators of glossy advertising.

When sellers want to appeal to your emotions, they will advertise their products in unfamiliar environments. If you don't believe me, check this week's Sunday supplements: the car is alongside some castle (you fancy the grandeur), or a wooden shack in some foreign land (you fancy the difference), or a deserted dock in run-down Liverpool (the contrast enhances the value of the car). If an unusual environment doesn't get to you, they assume that you are a (heterosexual) male and drape a near-naked woman over the bonnet to grab your attention, because market research shows that it works, at least on most men. (Recently, young men have begun to appear in these adverts alongside or instead of women, which suggests that marketing people are trying to grab the attention of an affluent sub-culture.)

Marketing people make their lucrative livings by knowing how to sell their client's products, and the fact that most advertising (though not all) appeals to fantasies, rather than addressing needs, ought to tell you something. By knowing what motivates most people, well-paid marketing people get it right more often than they get it wrong (which is why they are well paid) and, therefore, I conclude that most people buy cars for fanciful reasons. And as Jaws is likely to be more experienced at dealing with buyers motivated by their fancies rather than by their needs, it pays you to prepare beforehand to meet your needs and not your fancies. Thus, by sticking to your carefully thought-out needs, you get a slight edge as you play to the weaker of Jaws' strong suits.

If, on the other hand, you insist on buying a car for a fanciful reason – say, for personal image and prestige – your pursuit of image is more likely to make the car dearer precisely because this plays to Jaws' strongest suit: he is no longer selling you a car; he is selling you your self-image. In pursuing your fantasies, whatever they are, you concentrate on your fancies and not on the deal itself, and, believe me, Jaws notices this. It has long been honourable for sellers to exploit the fantasies of those with money to spend!

Thus, prepare for your next purchase by writing out the factual reasons for wanting a new car, and measure any and all cars against your criteria (is it big enough? will it start every time? etc.). This way, you won't buy just because Jaws discovers you fantasising about your fancies and manages to press the right 'buy button'.

Buyer psychology

It is not harder to buy expensive cars than it is to buy cheaper ones. The negotiating psychology is different, that's all.

In the economy end of the showroom, *Jaws will try to convince you that you can afford to buy one of his cars*, and he will offer all kinds of deals to make up any shortfall in your cash by:

- offering easy credit from a finance company (for which he gets an additional commission).
- allowing a trade-in price for your old vehicle (making a nice profit on the difference between what he allows you and what he re-sells it for).
- offering (only if pressed!) a small discount off the list price (or at least the list he shows you).

In the luxury end of the showroom, the entire psychology is reversed: *you feel obliged to convince Jaws that you can afford to make a purchase and you let him know that he is not wasting his time talking business with the likes of you.* Hence, you sell yourself to Jaws and he sells you an expensive car for your trouble. If it makes you happy, fine, but there is no reason why you can't get an expensive car at less than the first price Jaws thinks he is entitled to ask for.

Forgetting to Superdeal by concentrating on convincing Jaws that you are somebody of substance is a most expensive way to go about acquiring a luxury car. Your vanity allows Jaws to get you on the run almost before you have sighted the Mercedes that you intend to let him persuade you that you want.

The windscreen price

Car sellers splash their prices across windscreens in big type (anybody could pass a driving eyesight test if asked to read the price of a used car half a mile away). If it's not across the windscreen, but in a discreet little wooden holder placed on the bonnet (the prices of most Rollers are displayed in this way), the size of the type is in inverse proportion to the size of the price.

The price tag is there for a good (for Jaws) reason: if, having seen the price tag (and how can you miss it?), you keep talking, he knows the car can be sold at the asking price and, if he is really clever, at an even higher one using add-ons. *The windscreen price tag, in effect, is a trial close.*

What you need is a Superdeal strategy to take on the windscreen price when the chat gets down to money, for there is nothing sacrosanct about the price on the windscreen. It wasn't put there by Moses. It is merely the price that gives Jaws his most profitable mark-up. If he can get the windscreen price he is more than happy, and, therefore, he is only going to be slightly less happy if he is forced to cut it a little in order to sell the car. Whether you pay his best price, or his 'good enough' price, is up to you. Remember, you supply the car company's income by spending your own, and you have, or ought to have, some say in the outcome!

If Jaws deals in brand new cars, his mark-up (out of which he pays his costs and takes his profit) is about 18–20 per cent on factory prices. He boosts his mark-up by selling 'extras' (add-ons: 'entertainment' centres – i.e. radios – tinted windows, aluminium wheels, etc.) and also by conning you into paying more for absolutely nothing (of which more later). Hence, don't think you are home and dry if you accept the windscreen price – that is just the beginning of the sale.

If Jaws sells used cars, his mark-up can be anything from 40 to 60 per cent. His scope for padding the price is only limited by your own gullibility. The range of discount you can reasonably look for is clearly much greater than with brand new cars where dealer margins are tighter.

More than one price

Car prices vary between dealers and, obviously, between makes and models. At any one time, there are over 60,000 different makes and models of new cars on sale in the UK, and there are also many thousands of makes and models in the used car market, with wide variations in their prices depending on the cars' condition, age, the whims of the sellers and the innocence of the buyers.

Price lists for both new and used cars circulate in the trade. Basic prices for new cars are set by producers and their dealers, though these can and do vary. Used cars are more difficult to price, and many sellers use *Glass's Guide* to instil some (purely voluntary) regularity within the trade. This lists a valuation of each make and model of used car likely to be offered for sale in the UK, based roughly on its age, its apparent condition, its recorded mileage and the prices compilers of *Glass's Guide* observe in the market. *It is a guide, not a mandatory listing.* You can check the range of prices in used cars from the adverts in the local paper. Variation in price is caused partly by the unique condition of each used car – for instance, some rust faster than others – and partly by what the dealer thinks he can get for them.

Jaws judges (by listening to what you say and by watching how you say it) whether to price a used car at or above the top price quoted in *Glass's Guide*, or at or below its lower price. He then will offer a trade-in price for your old car to set against the basic price of the new(er) vehicle, dependent on how anxious you appear to be about a new car (this is where your fantasies let you down). Naturally, he will recoup any concessions he might have made to get you to buy the car at the (already high) windscreen price.

Knowledge of the *Glass's* price doesn't help you much. As usual, it's up to you to get a better price than the one you are first offered. For example, if you are offered, in an outburst of

Jeremiah pessimism, £2000 for your four-year-old compact, which *Glass's Guide* prices at £3100, and you foolishly accept this, Jaws will be able to realise the difference on the resale of your trade-in, adding to his profit at the expense of your generosity.

The only thing worse than parting with what Jaws described as an 'old wreck' for £2000 and, a fortnight later, finding it on his forecourt, spring-cleaned and looking its best, with a price sticker of £3250, is perhaps seeing Jaws taking off the sticker and shaking hands with a buyer, both of them grinning like Cheshire cats, though not for the same reason!

More profit from lending you money

Suppose, because your cash maximum plus the trade-in valuation is still below the windscreen price, you need credit to finance the new car. Jaws, of course, will be delighted to introduce you to a friendly (to him!) finance company to make up the difference. His personal commission from doing so is extra income, which Eezy Finance Ltd recoups in the money you give them while you repay the loan.

You can see why car salesmen are generally smiling from ear to ear as they go about their business! In fact, it is not quite clear why Jaws is selling cars for a living rather than the finance for you to buy them. He can make as good a living from his commission on arranging finance deals for you, so much so in fact that your efforts to buy a car for cash actually cause him to sweat in disgust at your sinful insistence on not going into debt to buy the car his way.

If you need finance of any kind, don't wait until Jaws sends you to Eezy Finance Ltd. *It pays to shop around.*

Try your bank first. In ascending order of expense to you, try for an overdraft and, finally, in desperation, a personal loan. Bank managers will offer to finance you in reverse order: a personal loan first and then, with reluctance, an overdraft. Why? Because banks make more money from personal loans than from overdrafts, hence, it is in your interests to try for an overdraft.

Finance companies are the most expensive way to borrow money. You can see this from the Annual Percentage Rate (APR) that they must display by law. Parliament decided that too many people were borrowing money without really knowing how much it was truly costing them, so they decided that all finance companies must inform borrowers what they charge for loans – the APR. This reveals the actual interest that you will be paying and, by rule of thumb, it is about twice the apparent interest rate they also display, usually in bigger type. Eezy Finance Ltd meets its legal obligations by printing the APR on its brochures and papers, but they are not required to hold a seminar in personal finance with you before you sign. If you don't know what the APR is, they are happy to leave you in ignorant bliss.

For an idea of the difference between the apparent interest rates and the APR, study the following table:

Apparent interest rate:	[10%]		[12%]		[14%]		[16%]	
Duration of loan (years):	2	4	2	4	2	4	2	4
Amount	Monthly payments (rounded to nearest £)							
£1000	50	29	51	31	53	33	55	34
£3000	150	88	155	93	160	98	165	103
£5000	250	146	258	154	266	162	275	170
Annual percentage rate (APR):	19.7%	19.0%	23.8%	22.8%	27.9%	26.5%	32.1%	30.3%

The bottom line shows you what you actually pay in interest on these borrowings. You should be able to do better with an overdraft.

Borrowers often suffer from the illusion that monthly payments are the sole criterion for deciding whether they can afford to buy something expensive like a car. People also make this mistake with mortgages. In the finance of any major item, there are three situations that you can find yourself in:

1. *You pay off the loan before you sell the car,* leaving you with the entire resale value as your equity that can then be applied to the purchase of another car (equity here is the same as it was for house equity).

2. *You sell the car and pay off the loan* and have some equity left over
   to apply towards another purchase.
3. *You sell the car and the price is insufficient to pay off the loan* (i.e. it
   has no owner's equity in it) and the debt is added to a new loan
   for the new car.

The first situation is preferable to the second and both are
preferable to the third.

The third situation is fairly common. People take on loans that
leave them still paying money back each month beyond the point
where the car (or yacht!) is worth what they still owe. They are in
the swamp, and if they don't get a grip on their debts, they go
under.

In almost all cases, people end up in a debt swamp because the
amount of the monthly instalments, or even their mere availability, were considered the decisive factor in going into debt.
The original loan is now a swamp, sucking them under. In
contrast, a swamp loan is a little goldmine for Eezy Finance Ltd,
which is seldom confused about anything to do with money.

The illusion of easy payments is best overcome by considering
what the loan is going to cost you in total – add the total interest
you are asked to pay to the original loan, and then compare this
with the car's likely value to you when you want to resell it.
Roughly, if a loan is for £5000 and the interest charge on £5000 is
£500 a year over four years, you pay £7000 for the £5000 motor
(4 × £500 = £2000). A check on the duration of the loan and
the likely fall in the value of the car (depreciation) will tell you if
you will get ahead or go under. When a car depreciates at 25 per
cent a year, the £5000 car is worth £3750 (£5000 minus £1250) at the
end of year 1; £2813 at the end of year 2; £2110 at the end of year 3;
and £1583 at the end of year 4. The used-car dealer estimates the
value to him of your car by making a calculation similar to the
above. You might get more, though I'd bet next month's drinks
bill that you'll get less.

Thus, if your loan is for £5000 for four years at 16 per cent
(30.3% APR), you will pay £170 a month for 48 months, or £8160
in total. When you try to sell the car at the end of the second year,
you know that it is worth about £2813, give or take a hundred or
two (perhaps Jaws is having an off-day or you get 'lucky' with
Tiddler), but you still owe Eezy Finance £4080. You're in the
swamp for about £1267 before you take out another loan.

Repeat this a few times over your car-buying cycle and you'll be
a favourite customer of the finance company – they'll keep
lending you money on cars and you'll keep getting deeper into
hock. They'll probably toast you at the Christmas party. Such a
status in the litany of heroes at Eezy Finance Ltd is not a great
credit for you, no matter how you tell it. It may have been
convenient to buy the car that way but it was hardly sensible.

Deciding whether to buy or not on the basis of whether you can
afford the payments without concern for the total amount you are
signing up for is a very expensive way to buy anything. The fact
that, in car buying, so many people get into the swamp is a
testimony either to mass gullibility on the part of buyers, or to the
supreme professional skills of the likes of Jaws.

Other rip-offs

The rip-offs don't stop with the finance. True, what follows can
be marginal compared to the high cost of borrowing money, but
any little nibble that Jaws can get away with, he takes out of your
pocket or purse.

To the basic price, Jaws adds the motor tax and the VAT. Fair
enough; after all, the government is entitled to its cut and there is
nothing anybody can do about it.

Maybe . . . but you ought first to find out what is included in –
and excluded from – the price on the windscreen. A tax-inclusive
price is a different proposition from a tax-exclusive price. VAT
alone will add 15 per cent to the purchase price of a new car, and
the question is whether this is paid by Jaws out of the sticker price
or whether it is added on top. Ask, and get a clear answer.

Now, if you co-operate fully with the Jaws road to riches, he
will go for the proverbial jugular. I refer to two items, beloved of
car salesmen, known as 'delivery' and 'number plates'.

The first is an absolute farce. They charge for 'delivering' the
car, and not too cheaply either: I've seen delivery charges of £150.
Ask them what this 'delivery' charge consists of and you get a
bewildering variety of vacuous replies. Basically, you pay for
them wheeling the car across the pavement out to the road, with
some preparation beforehand – a bit of cleaning and degreasing,
etc.

Recently, the combined effects of recession and competition have brought delivery charges down to below £50, and in fact, some companies now consolidate the charge into the windscreen price, enabling them to pretend that 'delivery' is 'free'. However, this will not stop this pernicious practice from reappearing at the first sign of a seller's market.

Whatever its price, 'delivery' is something you ought not to pay. It's a load of rubbish, devised in a previous age when sellers were thinking up 'add-ons' for a seller's market. Once the idea caught on, thousands of dealers copied it like demented junkies and it's been around ever since. *Superdealers never pay for a car dealer's 'delivery'!*

Following their success in getting buyers to pay for delivery, many dealers often charge for number plates too. It's a lucrative business for number plate manufacturers and for garages. Whether you pay or not (you shouldn't) depends on your buying strategy. It is to this that we shall now turn.

Clean up for the sale

If you are trading-in a car for whatever you think it is worth, it is worth a lot less in scruffy condition. So clean it up.

Some sellers tell you this is not important, but it is. Would you feel proud to buy a scruffy car that the owner has not even bothered to wash and sweep out? Sure, the dealer puts all trade-ins into the garage for a spring clean, no matter what condition they are in when they are bought, but a dirty car undermines any pretence, or even any true statement, that the car has been well looked after. Verbal veracity is always trumped by the evidence of one's eyes.

What is true for a dealer is true for a private buyer, only more so. Don't underestimate the intimidating influence of criticism – implicit or openly expressed – by family and friends on a buyer who drives home a mess ('what did you pay for *that*?') and, conversely, the effect on the buyer of anticipated praise for buying something to be shown off ('you *only* paid £5000 for it?'). So clean it up!

Minor maintenance and repairs should also be done at this time. All lights should be checked and any fuses or bulbs replaced. If anything is missing (a handle, a light rim, a wing mirror or a seat cover), replace it.

If the MOT is out of date, get one done, especially if you are looking for a private buyer. They like to drive off the car at the time of purchase, and the absence of an MOT certificate red-lights most buyers into wondering what needs to be fixed before the car is roadworthy. This puts pressure on your price, assuming, that is, they stay around to do a deal.

Therefore, you want that car to be looking its best when you run it up to Jaws for a trade-in or when showing it to private buyers answering your ad in the local papers.

Your buying strategy

You need a Superdeal strategy for buying a car. Don't just rely on an *ad hoc* adaptation to whatever happens when Jaws is sizing you up.

First, sort out your substantive reasons for buying a car. Write these down. These are going to determine why you do, or don't, want the car on offer. If two of you are going to use the car, make sure your partner's views count, too.

Second, decide how you are going to pay for your new car purchase. There are numerous combinations of ways that this can be managed:

1. Total price, cash down.
2. Some cash, plus finance.
3. Some cash, finance, plus trade-in allowance.
4. Finance only.
5. Trade-in only.

Third, decide whether to go for a dealer trade-in or a private sale, and certainly find out which is to your advantage in current trading conditions (including the condition of your car). In a private sale, you might be able to do better than in a garage trade-in. A well-kept, or cleaned-up, used car placed for sale in your local paper can raise you more cash than selling it to a dealer. Most dealers inspect trade-in cars with no less attention to detail than that used by St Peter at the Pearly Gates. Every single blemish, slight sign of a defect and missed note of the engine will be remarked upon, and with a performance (for that is what it is) that could win an Oscar, Jaws tells you his (low) price and that he doesn't mind whether you take it or leave it. One advantage with private buyers is that they are probably as unused to buying cars as you are and their scope for acting, in every sense of the word, like a dealer is much more limited.

Fourth, check the car showrooms and the local papers for details of cars that you might be interested in. Note their prices, and any special offers available to potential buyers like you.

Fifth, ignore the asking price; look over the car. If the price is not displayed, do not ask what it is at this moment. The car is probably looking spotless, which makes finding its blemishes a lot more difficult. Hence, look for them!

Visible items include:

- *condition of the body*
  dents?
  rust?
  scratches?
  evidence of repainting?
  anything loose?
  patches?
  broken aerial?
- *condition of the tyres*
  legal minimum tread?
  worn or new?
  matching pairs?
  spare OK?
- *condition of the engine*
  trial run it – hard!
  any odd sounds?
  date since service?
  battery levels?

- *condition of working parts*
  gears – work them!
  steering?
  brakes – slam them!
  lights all working?
  dashboard – missing lights?
  heating/ventilation?
  all windows working?
  all doors open and shut?
  boot opens and shuts?
  all keys working?
  radio working?
- *general condition*
  all seats functioning?
    (move them back)
  check under seat covers
  seat belts functioning?
  glove compartment operates?
  general appearance?
  tool kit in place?
  loose number plates?
  sunshades work?

Check everything off against a list such as the one above and visibly be seen to do so. Comment as you go through your checks on *any* defects, but don't wait for an explanation or excuse as to why bits won't work or don't look right.

'UNFORTUNATELY, NOW I'VE BOUGHT ALL THESE EXTRAS I CAN'T
AFFORD THE CAR ITSELF.'

Sixth, ask what the asking price includes ('on the road' or 'plus taxes, delivery and number plates'). You are looking for credible reasons not to pay the windscreen price, and to support what you want put right before you consider paying any price at all. If the seller makes any statement that this or that will be replaced or fixed, *write it down* on your list and make sure he sees you doing this. Your attack on the asking price begins with the defects that you have spotted.

Seventh, always demand a new set of tyres (including the spare) from dealers and do not be fooled by the black pitch with which they paint the outsides to make them look new. Demand a new battery, fan belt and plugs. If the MOT is close to expiring, demand they do an MOT at their expense. This tests their faith in the vehicle.

And, no matter how few or many defects you think you have found, demand 20 per cent off the asking price because of the 'poor condition' of the vehicle, reading specific defects from the list you have compiled as often as he tries to resist your challenges.

You can be sure that even if he does not give you a discount, he will make some concessions on the vehicle that he would not have made if you had simply accepted the price he first asked for. Anything you get off the price, or are given in lieu of a price cut, is to your advantage.

How to get the better of Jaws

Jaws will push down the trade-in price by finding excuses to pay under the odds, but as he is backed up by a garage full of mechanics who can put right minor blemishes in your old car in minutes, tell him to do so! As his mechanics are competent and have passed the car he is selling to you, surely their competence extends to fixing your trade-in?

Jaws always aims to recoup concessions he makes on your trade-in by sticking to the price he's offering for the car he is selling. He, of course, resists attacks on his prices. After all, over the years he has heard every objection there is, and with an almost bored air of indifference, he resists yours. He will tell you, *inter alia*:

Jaws	The truth
'The price is already discounted to take account of some of the things you have mentioned.'	Hardly likely; he hopes you will be like most others and be blind to blemishes.
'Our prices include a 12-month warranty on parts and labour.'	You pay the premiums for the group insurance cover for the warranty in the price, hence it's no concession to you (ask how much off for foregoing his warranty?).
'If I do *all* that you ask, I won't make a penny on the car.'	'If you don't do *some* of what I ask, you won't get a penny from me.'
'It's against company policy to alter prices in this way.'	'If you don't have discretion, let me speak to the guy who does.'
'Do you want the car or don't you?'	'That depends on your willingness to do a deal.'

His fightback against your price challenge is an attempt to intimidate you into accepting his price. Keep at it. He will either give in and give you a discount, or give you some other concession.

Jaws wants to sell you a car, and once he is convinced that you are serious about not paying his windscreen price, you can be sure that nine times out of ten he will do something extra to make you happy with the deal. He didn't get where he is by letting potential customers out of sight when a sale could be made if he made the effort. After all, ninety-seven customers out of a hundred never argue about anything and pay the windscreen price!

Things you need to know

To buy a car, there are three things you need to know:

1. Your maximum budget
2. Which car you like
3. What its on-the-road price is

Armed with this information, you open the negotiations with the dealer.

Psychologically, you need an edge, and you get one by being different from the normal car buyer who gets into a clinch with Jaws. Jaws ain't used to Superdealers; you ain't used to buying a car. His advantage in experience and practice over you is eliminated. That's your edge.

What are the differences between you and the average car buyer?

You know your cash limits. Having done your homework, you know the maximum budget you can afford to meet the price of the car you want. Note that your maximum budget implies nothing about how this maximum sum is financed; it merely gives you the total figure of cash you have, or can get, to buy a car.

If you are disposing of your old car, find out its worth. Ask garages to quote a cash price for it; check the local papers; consider selling it privately. Likewise, if you need finance, check what amount is available from your bank or a finance company. Compare this with what Jaws is offering. Do both these tasks before you meet with him to buy the car of your choice.

You choose a car you want to buy. To narrow the choice down to a specific car, or perhaps two, search the papers, read up on consumer surveys and visit dealers. In the search phase, ask questions about each type of car and note down on the brochures any features that might influence your choice, including the windscreen price, whether this is 'on-the-road' or 'in the show-room', any special deals going, and whether it is available from stock. Also acquire a brochure on the accessories that go with the models you are interested in.

You stay clear of opening any discussion about purchase until you are ready, and you refuse to be drawn into a negotiation. Merely state that you are collecting information, and if you decide something might be of interest, you will call back and talk to them about it. Relax Jaws by asking for his personal card and phone number, to facilitate contact when you return.

You do not dither nor do you disclose any confidences in your preparation for the negotiation. Jaws will try subtly to find out what you are up to, by building up your trust in him (fatal at this stage!). Are you a serious purchaser? He'll do a trial close: 'If this car can be supplied within your budget, will you buy it?' Tell him you don't know yet. How are you financing the purchase (cash, loan, trade-in)? Depends on what's the best deal. What car are you driving at present? Are you selling it? You don't know yet. When do you want to buy your new car? When you find what you want at a sensible price; otherwise, later.

You only make your negotiating move when you are ready. Are you ready? Let's go.

How to buy a car

Superdealers know which car they want before they meet Jaws for the price negotiations. They collect all the information they need about alternative cars in their survey of the market, and then have strictly separate discussions with the seller on selection of the car and negotiations to buy it. Combining the two discussions puts Jaws into the driving seat.

Don't open with any reference to how you intend to pay for the car you have decided to buy. When you pay cash, you are vulnerable (in the temptation sense) to the switch sale. If Jaws knows that you are paying cash, he knows that the cash you have, plus the loan he can get for you, enables you to buy a more expensive car, and he tries to persuade you to do so. The same is true if you are paying with cash plus a trade-in. A loan on top of the cash you have, plus the trade-in allowance, enables him to sell a more expensive car. Even when you decide to buy a car with help from a loan, he won't give up trying to switch-sell to a more expensive car.

For example, if the car you want is a Hondin 1.8 litre SG1 priced at £5000, Jaws will try to get you interested in the Hondin 2.4 litre GT3, a step or two up the same company's range, costing £6500. A car up the range always carries more attractive features than the models closer to the basic model. Ignore subtle hints about the inadequacies of the model you have chosen. If you don't and you bite, you'll pay more for your car:

'While the 1.8 Hondin is a perfectly good car – that's why we sell 'em – it may not quite be big enough/fast enough/roomy enough/stylish enough, etc., etc. for your needs [perhaps, identifying something you disclosed about your needs], and you might care to look over the 2.4 version.'

'You only get the power steering and the computer control system in models of this car above the 2-litre size.'

As he says this, he 'walks' you over towards the bigger car. Don't follow him: turn back and look inside the 1.8 model – he'll stop walking away and get on with selling the 1.8.

Tell Jaws firmly that you are only interested in the 1.8 and you'd like to discuss the price (mention the word *price*) and talk business. He has no option but to agree to do so. His preference, however, is to delay price negotiations until he has fully explored every option to sell you a more expensive car than your first choice. Be firm. He'll give in and talk about the 1.8 because, on the downside of the selling sequence, he prefers to sell *a* car to *no* car..

Set out your papers and the brochures you collected on the earlier visit. He reads upside down, will recognise the prices he quoted and will also note other writing alongside these prices (the special offers he, and other dealers, made at the time of your first forays).

Jaws will try to take command of the next ten minutes. Get in yourself – if necessary, interrupt him – and tell him:

(a) that you are ready to make a single firm offer for the 1.8 car he showed you.
(b) that it is for an on-the-road (no extras) price deal.
(c) that it is for immediate delivery.

Tell him: 'If you accept my offer of £. . . . , I am prepared to buy the 1.8 in the showroom today.' Then shut up and say nothing.

Jaws will shake his head, say 'No way', refer to list prices, tight dealer margins and 'my boss wouldn't let me sell the car under its maker's price.'

He isn't used to this approach. He normally takes command, finds out if there is a trade-in, quotes a low price for this whatever the make or model or offers a fixed price for any model, offers finance to an amount suited to the maximum payments you can make, and fills in an order form. By the time you can say 'I've been had again', he has your order ready for your signature without the slightest sign of a price concession.

Don't argue with his rejection of your offer. Repeat it calmly, and shut up and say nothing. Don't get drawn into the order-filling game. If he tries to get your name and address on to the form, tell him you will assist him with the order form when you have agreed the terms of business, but not before.

Jaws will repeat the first performance, perhaps with some new arguments ('the makers won't let us undersell other dealers'; 'we don't make a profit at that price'; 'the car is already heavily discounted to get the on-the-road price into it'; 'if you want to pay that price, I'd have to charge you for delivery, number plates and tax', etc.).

Repeat your offer calmly and shut up.

If Jaws asks any questions about the deal ('how are you paying for the car?'; 'is there a trade-in?'), it is a signal that he's thinking about how to squeeze something out of the deal for himself, i.e. he's sliding. It's called 'damage limitation'.

Tell him you want agreement on the price of your chosen car before you discuss how you want to pay for it. Try a trial close: 'who should I make the cheque out to?'. That will rattle him – you are no ordinary wally buying a new car!

Then shut up and say nothing.

Jaws has only two things he can do:

1. Say 'no' and mean it.
2. Say 'maybe' and try to move you up on price.

If a trade-in is involved, he will try to work on that price. Beware of an apparently high allowance appearing in the discussion. Quote him, if you are trading in your old car, his earlier offer for your car. If you are selling it privately, tell him there is no trade-in deal required. If finance is needed, he will try to work on the terms or the loan period to push up his 'take'. Tell him you have arranged finance elsewhere, or quote him his earlier offers on finance. This blocks off attempts to divert you into new pastures. You know your car, you know your finance, and Jaws knows you mean it.

He might try to intimidate you with a firm 'no' and terminate the discussion. You must be prepared to leave and go to another dealer.

Alternatively, Jaws might move on his price towards yours (no doubt huffing and puffing a bit). In response, you can move slightly up on yours but do not move much. You should have pitched your offer realistically and not have to shift it much.

If he does not move at all, you must not do so. Likely, he'll move slightly just before you drive off. You only move slightly in response to a move from him. You do not move unilaterally if he sticks to his windscreen price. If he says 'goodbye' in his office and lets you go, do so, perhaps walking round the 1.8 in the showroom one more time before leaving. In this 'game', you too can act.

But on your offer: sit tight!

Most times, Jaws finds a way to keep the deal alive. It will be below his asking price, though probably also above your offer price. You won't have been switch-sold, you won't have a phoney trade-in deal, you won't be in hock to an expensive finance company, but you will have the car you chose at a price close to one you can afford. That result makes you better off than 97 per cent of average car buyers.

You win.

Renting a car

Car, and yacht, rentals are open to Superdeals. Corporate discounts from the big car rental companies range up to 40 per cent off the hire charges they try to hit you with. There is loads of room for discounts, less onerous terms, better class of vehicle for a lower-class price and lower-priced extras. It's best to talk to the manager, as the counter clerks are addicted to written price schedules (it's their training). You have competition on your side – the hire firms run 'special deals' all the time and you are not in strange territory when you offer them one of your own.

A jump up in vehicle class, for instance, costs the rental manager almost nothing. It's standing in the carpark unrented, so why shouldn't she let it earn its keep from you? Another dodge is to keep on file all your car-hire paperwork, segregated by company (collect disused sheets from colleagues too). Approach the rental desk and open your file with a thick pile of forms and other headed paper from Hertzus, Avista, Fudgit, etc. Tell the clerk that you require a discount as a regular and loyal hirer. It doesn't matter if the paperwork is ancient or in somebody else's name; the evidence is compelling, and you'll get a discount, perhaps even a corporate one!

Apply the Superdeal principle: those who ask get (some of) what they want; those who don't, pay the tariff.

Your checklist

- Select factual criteria for choosing a car.
- Separate the search for a specific car from negotiations to buy it.
- Calculate your cash maximum from the sum of the cash you have available, the cash allowance for a trade-in or the private sale price for your car, plus any loan you arrange.
- Avoid loans that put you in a loan swamp.
- Clean up your car before you attempt to sell it.
- Select a specific car to buy.
- Don't allow a switch sale.
- Set a realistic price to purchase the car.
- Be prepared to look elsewhere if your offer is refused.

7

Buying and selling boats

Floating caravans

You don't have to be rich to be into boating (though some bank managers would argue that the two conditions are incompatible over the longer term), but if you do take to the sea, the financial strain is certain to cause you to give up a lot of other things. This is why boating is often described as a hole in the sea into which the owner pours money.

True, you can mess around in a little dinghy costing only several hundred pounds, but for a boat worth risking your life to sail in, you're into hock for many thousands more than you would expect to pay for a decent car. It's as if the volume car market started with a Mercedes and kept going past the Rollers from then on.

A yacht or boat is nothing more than a sea-going caravan. Next time you feel envious of people who own a lovely yacht, think of it on wheels, in front of you, on a narrow winding road, when you're in a hurry – it's the greatest cure for boat-envy there is! The market for nautical caravans is a mixture of the used car business and estate agency. The Superdeal skills you use in these markets are applicable, once adapted, to that for boats.

At any one time, there are many thousands of used boats for sale in the UK. The private owners' market is very active and you do deals with them in much the same way as for cars. Check the entire boat out thoroughly, hit them with your checklist and comment on every defect you find. Excuse nothing! And, of course, never praise the boat: all boats are *El Wrecko* (when buying).

Dealing with brokers

In the commercial market, the situation changes. Unlike with cars, where the dealer owns the vehicles, with boats this may or may not be the case. Some dealers buy boats and sell them, carrying the cost of their tied-up capital until they make a sale (you pay for the boat plus their selling costs). There are also brokers who act as agents – they don't own the boats they sell but act on behalf of their owners, charging various fees and expenses for doing so. This puts brokers in exactly the same position as estate agents – it is not clear on whose behalf they are acting, at least as far as sellers or buyers are concerned (that brokers look after their own interests goes without saying). Some brokers have a 'no sale, no charge' policy, but check out whether this applies only to the selling fee or to the ancillary, and necessary, expenses of advertising the boat and perhaps storing it as well.

The benefits of using a broker include their access to a wider market than would be produced by a few 'For Sale' notices on your local yacht club noticeboard, their professional expertise (invariably, brokers are keen boaters too) and their incentive to sell boats to make a living.

When considering the non-benefits, apply the same test as for house agents: much of what the broker does at your expense, you can do for yourself, especially in the case of advertising in the (numerous) specialist boating magazines (take a good photo, write a description and give a contact phone number: all boats are *El Spectacular* – if you're selling).

If the boat remains in your possession at your moorings, you will have to answer telephone enquiries, show people round and pay the bills associated with its care and maintenance. A local broker might help here if your boat is moored a long way from your home. He is available to show people around while you may have to keep them waiting a couple of weeks – and people buying boats, and much else, do not like to be kept waiting.

However, active brokers may have hundreds of boats on their books at any moment and yours may or may not get the attention it deserves. In addition, the temptation for a broker to 'switch-sell' upwards when somebody looks at your boat is not a figment of your paranoia. Sales commissions are related to the price the broker realises on all his boat sales. If you don't believe that this occurs, go to any broker and look at a middle-priced boat – you'll also be shown another boat at a higher price, and have to fight hard to keep your eye on the cheaper ones.

As with estate agents, you can expect calls from chancers who will offer to sell your boat to a 'Mr Ahmed' whom they know 'is in the market'. You know from the house market how to deal with approaches of this kind (sign nothing and tell them it's '*Habeas* Ahmed, or cast off').

When dealing with brokers, Superdealers find out exactly what they are to be charged in sales commission (if selling) and what all the extras are going to cost, including 'delivery' (if buying).

Superdealers – both buyers and sellers – work to lower the obligations the broker wants to impose on them. Remember: the broker's opening position is his best position, and he has a better-for-you position with less obligations but only if you push him to reveal it. So start pushing!

Twenty weeks' onshore storage at 'only', say, £12 a month adds £240 to your selling costs; delivery by road across the country is not cheap and by sea is even more expensive because of fuel, crew wages, food, etc. (never mind the fact that they thoroughly enjoy this kind of work, especially as they get a sail and you pay them too!). Either you pay these costs or the buyer does, depending on how keen you are to sell and he/she is to buy.

True, you face these costs yourself when you sell on your own account, but a broker can hide an additional profit mark-up in his 'reasonable' charges. He also receives the buyer's cheque, from which he makes deductions to cover his version of the agreed costs before passing the balance to you. If the boat remains unsold, he also has the boat, which is a powerful position to be in if there is an argument. Of course, all established brokers are generally honest and fair in their dealings, but there does not have to be intentional malfeasance present for disputes to arise over what was implied in the brokerage contract before you signed it.

Seasonal pressures

Boating, in the UK, is a seasonal activity. Winter on the North Atlantic is not the best time for a family outing (it's not the most favourite time and place for the professional seamen of the Royal Navy!). The seasonal nature of boating has an effect on the bargaining power of buyers and sellers.

Sailors like to sail. The one thing they can't abide is hanging about waiting to sail *if they have the prospect of getting to sea sooner*. That puts buyers in a weaker position when they rush into a purchase faster than they can tie a reef knot. With the thousands of boats that are for sale each day, you'd think that buyers would always be in the stronger position. So they would be, if only they'd not throw away their leverage in a bout of boater's insanity (it's not a clinical condition; it's just something else sailors catch – and it becomes terminal when they 'fall in love' with a boat they 'just have to buy'). Faced with a choice of a boat that is ready to sail at the start of the season, and waiting some months for the boat they really want, it's a half-shank to an outboard that they'll go for the immediate buy – and be willing to pay more for the privilege.

Buying a boat at the end of the season is tactically wiser than buying one at the beginning. Boats must be safely stored during the winter, and owners can only avoid these costs if they are sold at the end of the season. Prices tend to be softer, therefore, at the end of the season, and harder at the start. However, the lower price you pay or realise for a boat at the end of the season has to be balanced against winter storage costs and also the costs of making the boat seaworthy in the spring.

Finance

With boats costing upwards of £15,000 (£30,000 only gets you a fairly modest boat), the price ought not to be regarded as a *minor* hazard between the owner and the open sea. Unfortunately it often is, and the reason is not difficult to discover. Few people pay cash for their boats; most raise the finance from banks and specialist lenders. Naturally, many fall for the monthly payments error, as with houses, cars and other things. If they can afford the monthly payment, they tend to be careless about the interest they pay, the amount they borrow and the price they pay for the boat. Interestingly, some banks and finance houses place keen boaters in charge of their maritime lending operations on the principle that such employees can enthuse a willing borrower into a larger loan, and also that they will have enough boating sense to avoid financing an *El Wrecko*.

Dealers (clones of Jaws in the car-selling business, only more plausible, i.e. more gifted, in the disposing of *El Wreckos*!) are delighted to accept a cash deposit on a new boat (which isn't selling anyway – there's no 'rush hour' in a boatyard!) while you take a few weeks to raise the finance. For the sums involved (as high as £500,000), it can take weeks, particularly if you need to raise a second mortgage, while they check your status. Buyers who regard an allowance of time to raise the finance as a concession from the seller should recheck the price they have agreed to pay: it's probably too much.

Another 'dodge' (perfectly legal) is for the seller to allow you a generous trade-in on your current boat and then let you persuade him to accept it in lieu of a cash deposit on the new one. This way, he gets your boat on the market quickly and does not have to lay a penny out in cash. Meanwhile, you think you're smart because he's 'allowed' you six weeks to raise the remaining finance for the new boat. If anything goes wrong at your end, you've jeopardised your deposit (and don't have a boat), and he may have sold your boat at a profit to somebody else. He can't lose – you're tied into the sale whatever you do – and you can only win by going through with it.

Trade-ins and discounts

The other mistake buyers make is the usual one of the trade-in allowance on their current boat. In fact, the three-leg element of the boat sale – cash, finance and trade-in – work in exactly the same way as with cars – to the buyer's disadvantage. The 'generous' trade-in allowance is recouped either by the price you are charged for the boat or by the financial deal that is arranged with the 'friendly' lender.

Given that the official list prices of boats are about as reliable as a weather forecast, and the price discounts that sellers offer can be as spurious as the bark of a dog-fish, it is amazing that anybody takes prices seriously. *If you don't get 10 per cent discount off the seller's first price, you're obviously comatose – wake up and push harder and you'll get 20 per cent, minimum.*

You can do still better by getting between a builder and his dealers. A cash deal right in the boatyard, that cuts out the dealer's mark-up, could get you a 35 per cent discount off the so-called list price without sweat, providing you swear blind never to reveal this 'treachery' to his dealers. So swear! The obtainable discount tells you just how much the dealers mark up the boat builder's costs on the new boats they sell in their plush showrooms and moorings (the plusher their premises, the bigger their mark-ups). Buying from a dealer means that you're paying for his lifestyle – posh harbour premises, his own luxury yacht, etc. – and, therefore, you should be immune to his pleas of poverty and associated nonsense about 'tight margins'.

Make sure in your Superdeal with a seller that he remains responsible for defects found in the 'shakedown' first cruise – builders and dealers almost always agree to this for new boats – and get them to pay for delivery.

What's true for new boats is also true for used ones. A new boat depreciates something awful from the moment it slips from the dealer's mooring (it's their enormous mark-up over construction costs) and the used boat market reflects this situation, which is why many boaters only buy used boats in order to get more boat for their money.

Discounts are obtainable from used boat owners only if you ask for them. A boat is only worth what somebody is prepared to pay for it: remind the seller of this and go in well below his asking price. Every pound you get off the used boat price is money you can spend on doing it up, which is more than half the enjoyment about being into boating. When selling, only accept a lower price in exchange for less kit and spares on the boat – if they change the price, you change the package.

There never was a boat that required nothing doing to it, or which could not be 'improved' in some way by a new owner. If you ever come across a boat that you couldn't improve, or upon which you did not have an urge to spend more money, you are only kidding about being into boats, or have only been into them for ten minutes. You can spend a small fortune (and you will, you will!) on adding in auto-pilots, radar, searchlights, klaxons, VHF radios, echo sounders, winches, heaters, fridges, pumps, toilets, carpets, railings and nameplates, plus money on surveys, re-painting, cranage, harbour fees, fenders, safety kit, insurance and registration.

The prices of these and similar items are negotiable, so go about it in the Superdeal way (know what you want, search the market, demand a discount, and walk away if you don't get one).

Somewhere in the UK, any day of the week, any week of the year, a marine supplier will be selling the kit you need at a discount, *and that's before you've talked to him.* And you know what to do if he accepts credit cards.

In the unlikely event that you've found nothing else to do to the boat with your money, re-arrange the cabins, put more berths in or take some out, ditto with the heads ('toilets' to landlubbers), and galleys (kitchens!).

In between times, enjoy your sailing.

8

Complaints and remedies

What service?

Eating is hazardous. Somebody has shown, by force-feeding rats, that you risk cancer if you eat almost anything you enjoy. Hotels are hazardous. They burn down with alarming frequency and give you food poisoning. Like airlines, they are also often over-booked (I pass over the hazards of flying). Even if your favourite restaurant, hotel or airline has never let you down, you can bet your next hot dinner that they have let somebody down, just as you have been let down by other establishments (other people's 'favourites'?).

It is not difficult to find problems of bad service in any sector of our society. Indeed, as the leisure society develops out of afflu-ence, the problems of poor and inadequate service are bound to be a common experience for millions more of us. There just are not enough high-quality managements and staffs in the service sector to meet the (sometimes impossible) demands of the gen-eral public, more of whom every year discover the benefits of eating out, travelling about the world and resting up in four- and five-star hotels.

Poor and inadequate service is a common enough experience for most people, and how we cope with it is a fine test of our maturity. For example, everybody suffers at one time or another from assaults upon their desires, digestion and dignity by badly managed eating establishments. We all experience hotels that are like building sites, where the water runs cold if it runs at all and where the management disappear at the first sign that a guest might want something unusual, like a change of room, or even the room they booked. People who fly regularly have been made almost punch drunk by the way airlines manage their affairs (overbooking, lost luggage, cancelled flights, flooded toilets, no bar service, mixed-up reservations, etc.), and people who hardly fly at all must be bewildered and disillusioned.

The question is: *what do you do about it?*

So you think you've gotta problem?

The first thing you are going to have to sort out in your mind *before* you begin dealing with people responsible for bad service is: *what problem do you think you have?*

This is not always obvious. You may just be bad tempered about something else, or upset for a trivial reason. After all, if you think you've got problems with a badly managed restaurant, hotel, airline, theatre, government office, bank, building society, church, trade union, holiday resort or car-hire firm, how do you think the staff feel about working there?

So be clear about what the problem is, and be *very specific* about the problem you think you have. It's no good being vague or general: nail the real problem down. State it in a single sentence and avoid the temptation (and the Dutch courage of a dram too many!) to prepare sarcastic versions of your problem. Consider the following everyday scenes from a badly managed restaurant and some typical reactions of people exposed to them:

The problem	*Sarcastic response*
'I ordered my meal forty minutes ago.'	'If you take much longer, I'll die of starvation.'
'The wine has not yet arrived, and we've almost finished the main course.'	'Are you harvesting the grapes before you serve the wine?'
'I specifically booked a table in the secluded alcove and you have placed me next to the band.'	'If I wanted to join the band, I'd have learned to play the trumpet.'
'This bill includes items I did not order and prices higher than those shown on the menu, and it is added up incorrectly.'	'Are you trying to rip me off?'

Sarcasm is no way to handle a problem, even though you may get some enjoyment from it. It is difficult to resist being sarcastic when you have a small audience – your guests – and a few drinks inside you. But there is nothing more likely to lead to a row, and a failure to put right what is wrong, than an emotional outburst by an aggrieved customer.

By being specific, Superdealers refrain from diluting the power of their legitimate complaint. Including anything in your complaint that is not strictly relevant risks a happy diversion into challenges as to your seriousness by an harassed management. Sarcasm bites – but those who are bitten often bite back!

What do you want done about it?

Deciding this is the important step for, without action, all else is of no material value whatsoever. The problem inflicted upon you by the management and staff of the company you have been dealing with has undoubtedly annoyed, perhaps even humiliated you, but if nothing is done about it, all you are left with is a distasteful memory of an emotional row, which is neither satisfying afterwards nor compensation for your grievance (unless you thrive on exhibitions of emotional immaturity).

Superdealers concentrate on the remedy, not the grievance.

What *specifically* do you want done about your specific complaint? Now, bear in mind three things when deciding on your proposed remedy:

1. Your remedy must be within the gift of the management.
2. You must be realistic as well as specific about what you expect them to do.
3. You must be prepared to tell them what you want and not leave them to guess what will satisfy you.

In the absence of a proposed remedy, the management have to judge what will satisfy the complainer. Depending on the problem, the company has a number of responses, running from an apology to a refund. Indeed, some large companies employ 'customer services' departments to conduct correspondence with aggrieved clients.

By proposing a remedy yourself, especially in the immediate

situation of the restaurant, hotel, aircraft or whatever, you relieve the management of having to make a guess, and you also divert the staff from defending their honour and status in a blazing row with you. People who serve the public are under considerable pressure from all quarters: customers demand immediate service from them, while the responsibility for any delay may be caused by somebody else; as they are the nearest representatives of the company, aggrieved customers blame and criticise them. While this can cause them to react emotionally to a general complaint, a realistic remedy defuses tension and helps both parties.

How to propose a remedy

Remedies come in all sorts of guises, tangible and intangible, costly and *gratis*, immediate and delayed, satisfying or frustrating, real or imaginary, morale-boosting or face-saving.

Starting with the easiest remedy to receive, note the power and the simplicity of an apology: it meets some part of your needs and is the least costly all round.

Apologies are second nature to badly run businesses – after all, they get plenty of practice at apologising if their standards of service are generally poor. Well-managed hotels are always embarrassed when they have to make an apology, for they are not used to the experience. *Hence, your minimum expectation is an apology.*

Hopeful diners who say things like 'The least you can do is apologise' and then pause for the manager to say something like 'The least is not enough – have a drink on the house' are likely to be disappointed. If you only mention your expectation of an apology, that is all you will get. Instead, if you are looking for more than an apology and it is appropriate in the circumstances that you do so, tell them what you want in recompense for the trouble they have caused you and your party:

Remedy	Comment
'I suggest that a free round of drinks will make up for the excessive time we have been kept waiting.'	'Suggest' has a soft tone and is likely to get a positive response if the delay has been inordinate.

Remedy	Comment
'Because of the delay in delivering the wine to the table, I suggest that you send across two bottles and only charge for one.'	Restaurant wines are over-priced and they will recover the cost if you order more than two bottles later.
'The main courses were not cooked to our orders, so I suggest that you send across the sweet trolley and let us choose without charge.'	Portion sizes are not exact, and they can recover costs easily.
'The evening has been a minor disaster and you should order and pay for our taxi home.'	Acceptable, providing you don't live too far away.
'This bill is so badly put together that I suggest you send across a complimentary box of After Eights while we sort it out.'	Good move with waiters who can't count.
'In view of the disaster to my wife's/friend's main course and dessert, I suggest that you present her with a bouquet of flowers before we leave.'	Strong move when your companion is good looking or old enough to be your mother (waiters are incorrigible chauvinists!).

All of these remedies are well within the power of the establishment to supply. ***Superdealers don't waste time moaning; they propose a remedy!***

Suppose you require a cash discount instead of a free gift. You can go for this remedy, especially in hotels and places where free gifts are not obvious or are too trivial in the context of the problem you experienced. In ascending level of the seriousness of your grievance and, therefore, the severity of your remedy, you could try a version of one of the following:

Remedy	Comment
'If I am ever to stay here again, you should re-present an adjusted bill for much less than the amount shown on this one.'	A weakish move: it uses an implied threat that may not impress a busy hotel and leaves the size (if any offered) of adjustment to the hotel.
'To make up for what we have suffered, I *suggest* that you take 5 (10, 20, 40) per cent off the bill.'	'Suggest' is weaker than 'demand' but probably easier for beginners to say without flinching.

Remedy	Comment
'In view of the complaints from my wife/husband/friend, I *require* a refund of £30.'	With practice, you will use this tougher, but not offensive, language.
'I am deducting the room and service charge from the account because of the inconvenience you have caused to my party.'	Unilateral action escalates the tension and must only be used when you can do so without retreating.
'Things have been so bad tonight that I do not expect to be presented with a bill at all.'	Extreme position, just short of refusing to pay (a high-risk move), and leaves next move to the establishment.
'There is no way I will pay for the room you booked me into.'	You must be able to show that your actions are not only fully justified – *get witnesses* – but that, if pressed, you intend to fight it through the courts. But if you can't pass a breath-test, watch it, and even if you can, the staff will swear that you were blind drunk (so get more witnesses!).

If the service is haughty, pompous and slovenly as well as peccadillo-ridden, you should approach the manager. Remember that calmness in the presentation of your grievance and your remedy is much appreciated by managers. It ensures that the presence of an unhappy customer is not advertised to others in the restaurant/hotel/check-in/store (of course, you can use a louder voice if they are being unreasonably obstructive). Managers like to manage. They like to demonstrate their power of being able to put things right. Unfortunately, they also regard criticism of their domain as a personal slight.

Managers do not always have discretion over company policy. Sometimes, they have rules (or they tell you that they do) that prevent them from responding to your remedy. For example, they may not be able to ring up prices on the till that do not correspond to the prices on the menu (used by chain hotels to prevent staff fiddling the till money). In this case, suggest that they ring up three soups instead of a discounted steak.

Employees know the kinks in their employer's systems and

you can be sure that they can meet your remedy, often without their boss knowing. A waiter can, for instance, adjust your bill by quite substantial amounts, or give you items from the menu without charge, in pursuit of that grail of happiness that emanates from a previously unhappy customer who has been 'fixed' after specific complaints!

Proprietors do not like to be made fools of in front of their staff or other customers, and nothing is more likely to serve you poorly in pursuit of your interests than forgetting this point.

9

Travel and holidays

The Scottish author who said it was better to travel hopefully than to arrive missed by several decades the joys of hanging around an airport waiting to get going, never mind arrive there. If your travel plans are down to hope only, you are in for a stressful and tiring journey.

Travelling on business is no fun. After the first two dozen trips to Hawaii, even a sales conference in Birmingham can begin to look attractive. However, a holiday that involves travel has one compensation: the atrocities of the journey can be soothed on a sunny beach and forgotten after a bottle or two of the local nectar.

With hotels you are similarly at risk. You are dependent on the services of others, not all of them well disposed to you and your interests. Whenever your interests are at stake, you need Superdeal skills.

Coping with hotels

Hotels come in all shapes and sizes, and the service in them varies remarkably too. You can get pretty tatty service in some five-star hotels (on a bad night) and some marvellous service in a run-down slum. It's not easy to predict from the outside what the service is like inside. Three- and five-star hotels are supposed to be of a high standard but, once inside the rooms, you may find traces of the previous barbarians who stayed there that are visible to the most myopic of glances.

What do you do when the hotel and its services are not quite what you thought you were paying for? Well, you can draw up a list of complaints. But, as usual, what good does that do you? They may be proud of, or indifferent to, the kinds of things that you believe are unacceptable.

The only way to get anything done is to tell the management exactly what you want done about it – that is, propose a reasonable remedy. If the room is unsuitable (too small, too cold, too damp, too smelly, too far from the lift, etc.), it's no good just telling them that you are unsatisfied. Tell them that you require your room to be changed to another one. In almost all imaginable cases, they will do so. One room is much like another to the front-desk clerks: they did not prepare it, and they might have a dimmer view than you of those that did (there are no secrets among the staff of hotels, and even well-managed hotels are riven with rivalries). They can also arrange to replace TVs, bed linen, lights and such like without fuss. They don't have to do it themselves – they call the porters, or the chamber staff – and they will probably agree that the chamber staff need chastising on occasion.

A row at reception the morning after about the state of the room is almost too late, and it's often counter-productive. This is when desk clerks are most under pressure with people checking out, and they are less inclined to remedy a defect, principally on the grounds that, if you slept through it without a complaint, it could not have been that serious.

You are in your strongest position in the first hour of your presence in your room. All defects that you require to be put right are also more easily attended to at that time than after midnight. If the TV is not working, and you want to watch it (you're paying for it), it's better to call reception as soon as you spot the fault and not several hours later. Videos in the room often cause problems because earlier guests have been mucking about with the controls. Reception may not know of this, so tell them you want it fixed. As you pay for these services in your room charge, their absence is a justifiable case for a discount.

Perhaps the hotel cannot fix things to your satisfaction – there are no other rooms available, the maintenance engineer has gone home, there is a fault in the electrical system beyond their control. You can press for an alternative as compensation – free drinks in the bar, a meal in the restaurant, phone calls at Telecom, not hotel, rates, etc.

By concentrating on your remedy, you are halfway to achieving it.

When your room service breakfast is so late that you are in danger of missing your appointment, require the hotel to provide a taxi at their expense to get you wherever (within reason!) you're going. When your meal is served ages after you ordered it (kitchens do forget meal orders sometimes, or one waiter will serve another waiter's order to somebody else's table), ask for a free bottle of wine to cheer you up, or a discount off the bill. When the room fittings are not working properly – showers without controls, cold water in the bath, permanently running toilets, power points on the blink, trouser presses that don't and hair-dryers that scald – require a single-room rate charge instead of a double, or a straight cut in the bill.

Many hotels separate their functions into different accounts. For example, the banqueting manager may have no authority to cut your room rate because of bad service in his department. However, the general manager has, so ask for him, and do so when you want a concession in the reverse direction.

When booking hotels, remember that the business is very competitive. Ask for the single-room rate first and check what is included in it. Then go for a discount for staying more than one night and offer to eat in the restaurant if they give you one (the restaurant mark-up can be as high as 4000 per cent in central London). If staying more than one night with someone else, go for a single-room rate for the two of you, and then (if appropriate) get your kids' accommodation thrown in free.

Hotel phone charges are the greatest rip-off since Al Capone: they are often twice or more the Telecom rate. You can trade this charge down if you are staying more than one night, and you certainly can if you are a regular customer of the hotel or the chain to which it belongs.

No hotel manager who has ever lasted more than a week in the job will refuse some kind of discount to get your business, with the sole exception of when the hotel is fully booked in the high season. An empty room earns nothing but costs the same as a full one. Unused services earn nothing, but the staff who supply them still get paid for being there. This is your access to leverage, providing that you don't get greedy and demand the entire hotel's services for next to nothing.

Hotel managers haggle with suppliers all day long. A haggle with a customer is unusual (most people pay the list prices) but it is not so alien to them that they will say 'no' and mean it. They know that you can go elsewhere, but they prefer you to spend your money with them. What they 'lose' in a room discount, they hope to gain in the restaurant or bar.

Many hotel chains are now so desperate to get your business and to build up on customer loyalty that they offer all kinds of inducements (charge cards, rapid check-out, weekend breaks, special offers, prizes and competitions, etc.). Superdealers collect these inducements and select from among them the best deal available for the accommodation that they want.

Ringing up a hotel for which you have a 'privileged customer card' can get you a better room than you were looking for at a lower price. Work your way through the 'privileged cards' for each chain until you get the best deal in town for that night, not forgetting to cancel all the other reservations – 'you've been called away by your company', etc.

In hotels, as in much else, it pays to shop around. So do so, and with the savings you make, you can afford a better claret than the house red they were about to serve you, or a nicer present for your spouse than the one you intended to take home.

How to get by when you fly

The biggest problem with air travel isn't the occasional accident, bad as this is for the unfortunates who experience it. No, the biggest problem is that air travel is less immune to cock-ups than almost any other mode of getting from one place to another devised by human ingenuity.

Every hour of every day, there are millions of people in planes, getting off or on them, and waiting about airports with one eye on the indicator board and the other on their luggage (which is why there are so many cross-eyed air travellers around). Add to this the queues at customs and immigration, the crowds around baggage reclaim areas and the taxi, rail and bus ranks, and you have all the ingredients for an economy-class snarl-up.

It's amazing that more doesn't go wrong, though when it goes wrong for you, it ain't going to make you feel any better if it goes

wrong for others, too. Missed connections, delayed flights, lost luggage, cancelled confirmed reservations, changes in destination (and not just by hijackers), flights without food, dry bars, strikes and go-slows (if you can spot the difference), emergencies of any kind, a massed influx of people from previously cancelled flights and so on, all these are sufficiently regular events for one or more of them to affect you and your travel plans eventually.

Most of the time, there isn't a lot you, or anybody else, can do about it.

Faced with a mob of irascible travellers (and everybody is irascible when inconvenienced at an airport), the ground staff develop glazed looks in their eyes, go semi-catatonic, hide behind their passenger-proof desks and count the hours till their shift ends. There are always a few passengers who assert their rights by shouting loudly. Some even turn to violence and have to be restrained by gorillas out of airport security, a tactic best avoided in some of the world's airports where the paramilitary have not heard of the Geneva Convention and apparently don't take prisoners, or if they do, you'll wish they hadn't.

Those who fly regularly – the 100,000 miles-a-year club – have been well worn by experience. They know that the chances of something going wrong at some time on some flight or other are slim, but not slim enough that the prospect of some inconvenience can be disregarded. Veteran air travellers develop a stoicism about delays, disruption and disaster; if they don't, they end up in another job that doesn't involve air travel (usually after a valedictory tantrum at the check-in).

Scheduled flights that fail to go or to arrive on time are not, contrary to the illusion of some passengers, a breach of the UN convention on human rights (read the small print on your ticket). These are no different from any other failure of a supplier to meet the agreed terms of doing business with you, and are, therefore, open to the usual remedies.

Blasting the ground staff is as pointless as blasting the driver of the butcher's delivery van who has not been given your full order, or blaming the telephonist for the contents of a phone call, or the government for the weather. If a supplier fails you in some respect, the remedy you require is obtainable from those responsible for the business, i.e. the management. The lad or lass on the ticket desk has no authority to reimburse you for a missed connection, nor to compensate you for some failure of the airline (they are not responsible for the failure either!), nor to pay consequential damages arising from events beyond the airline's control (*'force majeure'*).

Superdealers direct their complaints and the remedy they require to the responsible level of authority.

In doing so, Superdealers make sure that the failure is a genuine responsibility of the airline and not a consequential failure resulting from some other party fouling things up. Airlines are not responsible for air traffic controllers, the weather, emergencies in other airports, military coups, wars, invasions, plagues, traffic jams outside the airport (or inside it) or earthquakes. There is absolutely no point in berating conveniently accessible airline staff just because the inconvenience that you are suffering is of a grievous nature. First, find out what the problem is; second, what is causing it; and then, and only then, consider the options that you have – alternative arrangements, realistic remedies or, *in ultimo extremis*, stoic acceptance of your fate.

On those occasions where the airline is definitely at fault, or where it can take responsibility for your innocent plight, you can work out a realistic remedy that meets some of your needs. For instance, if the airline has overbooked the flight and, despite your confirmed reservations, denies you passage (perhaps the most outrageous and unacceptable treatment you can receive – over-booking ought to be made a crime in my view), you can demand a 'denied boarding compensation' payment and, if there are conse-quential delays (an overnight stay, etc.), you can demand full use of local hotel facilities (including free telex, telephone and courier services). When the airline loses your baggage (a frequent occur-rence for the frequent traveller), you should contact the airline's representative at that airport, initiate the procedures to retrieve your baggage from wherever it went, and insist on his or her presence by your side until the bag is traced. When caught short with nothing but the clothes you flew in, you can require a replacement set of toiletries and, where plausible, an allowance to purchase a reasonable change of clothes while you go about your business (go for $150 as a minimum).

Almost all airlines, if required, meet reasonable claims, and the ground representative is more likely to be willing to do so (he or she has the authority and a small budget for these emergencies) if you treat them with respect, but firmly. However, don't go off the deep end while engaging them in negotiation.

An airline that diverts your plane to another airport can be required to notify, at their expense, people you were expecting to meet. A sudden uproar at the news on your part may make you look very foolish when you find that the diversion is caused by a serious accident at the airport to which you were booked to travel – after all, your inconvenience is a small discomfort compared to the poor souls ahead of you and, if given the choice, I'm sure you would rather not swap places with them.

An airport closed by bad weather is an unsafe one to land in; an aircraft diverted because of an on-board emergency is better on the ground in the wrong place than one that carries on and takes risks with your safety. A flight diverted by a hijack is an occasion to keep your mouth shut and your criticism to yourself – hijackers are not the most patient of people with pompous, loudmouthed critics.

Does this mean that you accept whatever is doled out to you in the flying stakes? In one sense, it does. Much that goes wrong with your flight plans cannot reasonably be remedied by those whose business it is to fly you to your destination. On the other hand, where things can be remedied, Superdealers seek out the reasonable remedy and get to the managerial level that can approve it.

Failures in service by an airline are not lightly regarded by the staff, unless by your insults and behaviour you give them reason to resist your legitimate demands. A cheerful complaint *plus a reasonable remedy* (a free drink, a movement up in the class of travel, etc.) directed quietly at the appropriate person can achieve wonders. A sour-faced howl, directed at those who are not responsible, and threats of dire consequences when you get home, only encourage the staff to leave you to stew in your misery. The aircrew did not lose your bag, they did not cause you to miss your connection, they did not overbook nor did they speak rudely to you on the previous leg of your journey. While this was going on, they were probably in bed or getting ready for their flight.

You'll move from economy to business class, or business to first class, faster with the crew on your side than you will with them ranged against you. It costs them nothing to move you up a class, and if your predicament is genuine and your remedy for it reasonable, you can bet a scotch to some champagne that you'll be sitting more comfortably elsewhere sooner than it takes the drink trolley to get to you, which, no matter where you sit, always starts serving somewhere else.

Dealing with travel agents

The holiday travel business is pretty well organised by the tour operators. They sell their fixed price 'packages' using mass market techniques. If they get it right and bookings are strong, there is not a lot of room for a negotiation. Thankfully, they often get it wrong (wrong price, wrong countries, wrong packages) and they are forced to slash prices and offer side deals to get any custom at all.

Hence, booking a holiday early on in the year is daft. You are almost certain to pay their list price, though they may offer to hold their prices as an inducement. But remember, they have the use of your money while you're waiting to get to the sunshine (advance payment discount?), and the promise not to surcharge you for fuel costs and airport taxes is hardly proper compensation.

It's better to book later, when the trends in the holiday market are made public (watch TV for the regular holiday programmes that provide information as well as ideas about where to go and what it costs).

Walk down any High Street and see what is on offer. When bookings are weak, they try offering cut price deals to make up the numbers. These can be twenty per cent below the price the early bookers have paid, or they can run on your holiday for an extra week at purely nominal cost because the following week is underbooked.

If this is not enough to fill up a quota, the early bookers are likely to find themselves diverted to another destination on arrival, much the same as happens when the local hotels have overbooked. The same remedies apply.

It is not uncommon for package tours to be diverted on arrival because the hotels concerned have (like the airlines) overbooked without informing the travel agency in charge of your holiday. The travel people try to redirect their clients to alternative resorts, sometimes miles away from where you expected to be staying.

Superdealers listen first to the alternative proposals offered by the company. They don't explode in rage before they have heard what is on offer. I've been met by a travel agent in France full of apologies at a sudden change in venue and, on listening to what they were offering, realised very quickly that it was a better deal than the villa I'd booked (swimming pool, more rooms, same charge).

At a minimum, if unsatisfied, you can require a discount of some kind (they pay for the car hire, the taxi ride, the first night's meals or a case of wine). Where the alternative accommodation is genuinely of a lower standard, you can require a discount off the cost of the holiday from the company that sent you there. They might say 'no' or, worse, ignore your letters. Persist. See the top management, keep your reasonable demands to the fore and your emotions in the background.

Local agents in these circumstances do have authority to make deals with you. If they want to send you to Corfu instead of Zakinthos, you have a number of strategies: a large discount on the Corfu trip; a 'special price' for a trip to Zakinthos; a free weekend's or night's accommodation in a five-star Athens hotel; a refund on the holiday; or a discount on another holiday later in the year. Certainly, they should pay for phone calls to your relatives and friends to notify them of the change in venue. You can also require them, for instance, to use their money to pay the cost of a higher-class hotel in Zakinthos, and you can offer (reluctantly) to make up the difference.

The market in cancellations is a source of cheaper holidays. Early bookers do change their minds, for all the usual reasons. They lose their deposits, and sometimes they lose the entire cost of their holiday if the cancellation is very close to the departure date. Walk into the agency and be ready to go at a few days' notice and you can walk out with a fabulous holiday at a nominal charge – first class hotels in the USA etc. for £80 a week; a deck cabin cruise of the Caribbean for £100 etc.

You can look for these deals providing you have flexibility. Try the newspapers. Why not ring round all the agents in the Yellow Pages and ask if they have any cancelled holidays for sale? Note them down, compare the list and then choose, asking for an extra discount as a matter of course!

The secret of negotiating against fixed prices in the holiday business is to do so at the appropriate time – when you have leverage, which is usually closer to the departure date than when the glossy brochures go out in January.

With airlines, a much crazier fixed price system operates, at least that is how it appears. Airlines seldom carry a plane load of passengers who all pay the same price. There can be a dozen different prices for tickets for any dozen passengers.

Scheduled prices, usually fixed by the aviation authorities, are paid by some passengers. There is a lot of scope here for negotiation, providing you can find the right people to negotiate with.

Travel agents get a commission off the price of the ticket you pay for booking you on that airline. If you do a lot of business with

an agent, you can get a share of that commission. Businesses get
large discounts for their frequent use of an airline, and travel
agents are only too pleased to arrange this. Their inhibition in
sharing their commission with you for arranging your holiday in
Majorca is not unconnected with their interest in their own
profitability.

Competition is your best weapon. If they don't sell travel, they
don't stay in business. They may not be willing to write a ticket
down in price – the airline reads all tickets when it calculates
agency commissions! – but they can give you a cash refund across
the counter, or arrange some other benefit for you (better hotel,
better exchange rate, phone calls to book a hire-car).

Look in the papers and see what the 'bucket shops' are asking
for selling scheduled tickets to your destination. Airlines sell as
many scheduled tickets as they can at the official price, but they
know also that for certain flights in certain months they cannot fill
all the seats at those prices. Hence, they sell off, at a massive
discount, a proportion of tickets for those flights to so-called
'bucket shops' (through intermediaries, so as not to directly
offend the regulations or compromise their spurious claims to sell
only at fixed prices). These tickets are then on the market at a
fraction of the full price cost. You buy them and the airline fills the
plane.

There is no point being nervous about using 'bucket shops', for
the economics of this practice make sense. Once a plane has filled
some proportion of the seats at full price, every other passenger
on board is pure profit to the airline. That is why they have 'stand
by' fares at airports, and that is why they deal with 'bucket shops'
(though they pretend not to). A plane with forty per cent of the
passengers paying the full fare of £600, twenty per cent paying
£400, ten per cent paying £260 and thirty per cent empty is far
more profitable for the airline than a half empty plane with full
fare passengers only.

Search for the discount fares travel specialist in your area. See
what he has got to offer and try him out on a trip. Once you get to
know the business you can negotiate even better deals with him,
for you can bet a week-end in Paris to a round the world trip that
his mark-up on the 'bucket' price is not less than 100 per cent.

10

Dealing with other people

I once met an American professor who remarked that he never ceased to be sceptical of people who knew what was good for the population of Vietnam (or, by extension, the United States) but who were pretty poor judges when it came to handling their own personal lives, especially when another human being was involved.

The paradox is not uncommon: London, for instance, though not exceptionally, is full of people who love humanity and hate each other. The hatred that zealots reserve for dissidents within the religious or political sect to which they subscribe is more strident than anything they display towards their enemies across the ideological divide.

Other people are among nature's most perplexing of creatures. Unless you are a recluse, you must deal with them. There is no alternative in the normal lives of normal people, and certainly not in our interdependent affluent society.

Superdealing has a role to play in helping you to cope with others, not the least by helping you to help them cope with you!

Dealing with household help

Californians (or at least those on TV cop shows) often claim: 'You get what you pay for.' In the household-help market, however, this may not be true.

Some people go through more daily helps, gardeners and au pairs in a year than others in a lifetime and they often explain their attrition rate by reference to the 'fact' (and they believe it is a fact!)

that 'dailies' and others, unless carefully watched, are untrust-
worthy or worse. The fact (and this *is* a fact) that other people
keep the same daily help year after year, without traumas and
upsets, does not appear to register a⁊ other than the 'luck' of the
draw: those who keep the same daily obviously found a gem;
those who frequently lose theirs are still searching.

*For Superdealers, success in the daily-help market is fully
explained by the way that household help is managed and
rewarded.*

The modern daily, thankfully, is not under the same pressures
and strict controls of the Edwardian household servant. In those
days, the servants were managed by the head butler. He hired
and fired (and often abused) those who worked for low wages in
the large establishment that was his domain. The master or
mistress of the house seldom interfered; if they did, they under-
mined the entire system of docility and obedience, and strict
sense of rank and order, upon which the accomplishment of the
household tasks depended. The butler did not regard himself as a
'servant' and certainly not of the same status as the servants he
managed, a point poignantly made in J. M. Barrie's play, *The
Admirable Crichton*. In this, the eponymous hero told his master
that it wasn't the thought of himself being regarded as an equal to
his lordship that disturbed him about the notion of equality, but
the thought that the servants would regard themselves as an
equal to himself.

Those who would manage household help should know that
their dailies have attitudes closer to Crichton than to those of a
'servant' – in short, they are more snobbish than subservient. In
almost every case that I have observed, any trouble with dailies,
gardeners and au pairs almost always comes down to the way
they are treated, implicitly and explicitly, by those who hire their
services. The modern household daily resents being treated as if
they are a menial hireling at the beck and call of somebody visibly
feeling superior in every respect. They see the insides (and
backsides) of the houses in which they work and don't take
kindly to being put in their places by out-of-work slave drivers.
Either they are treated with respect or they deliberately foul up
their domestic tasks until they quit or get fired.

There must be something about the necessity of domestic help
that brings out the worst in otherwise quite liberal and generous

people. Perhaps the householders feel guilty, or perhaps, more likely, they feel superior because they are hiring help and not having to do it themselves. Treat your help as if he or she were a snob, assuming that you find it impossible to treat them as an equal. Play to their snobbery and their pride and you will get more out of them than you would otherwise.

A gardener, for instance, is employed to work in the garden, manage it through the seasons, use gardening skills acquired by experience and make the necessary decisions about when and in what order to do things that need to be done. Right? Well, let him get on with it. Don't downgrade him into a mere garden labourer, prevented from exercising initiative and forced to adjust to your fantasies about what the garden needs. If you hire a labourer to cut the hedge, and clear up afterwards, give him the tools and go away and do something else. If you need a tree surgeon to develop your hedge, or trim the trees, you would not expect to have to tell them how to do whatever it was you wanted.

In single, one-off, jobs like these where the end product is visible – either the hedge is trimmed or it isn't – pay for the work to be done and not for the hours it takes someone to do it. If they do it in half the time you thought they would, so what? How people use their skills is none of your business. If you feel you have overpaid them, put it down to experience (yours as well as theirs).

A garden that needs to be completely redone, which you don't have the time or the skills to do yourself, can be brought up to your standards by regular work for a few hours a week by a professional gardener. Hire him to get on with it. If the hourly rate is attractive to you, pay it and stand back. His professional pride, and the initiatives you allow him to take, will do more for the outcome of his efforts in your garden than running round with a stop watch and closely interrogating his every move.

With domestic help, it is no different. You need help for some good reason (or, perhaps, you don't want to do the work anyway), so before you hire someone to carry out these agreed tasks on a regular basis, decide beforehand exactly what you want done each week or month and discuss this with the person concerned.

It's no good listing every single household task you can think up and then expecting a part-time daily to dash round the house like a greyhound doing them. The workload has to be reasonable, or it won't be done, and you'll spend a lot of time and energy hectoring the lady about her failings. She will resent this – and you – and will demonstrate just how little can be done in a long time.

Superdealers decide what reasonable workload can be done by someone, secure their agreement to do it and leave them to get on with it.

They do not time their domestic help's every arrival and departure. If the daily finishes the tasks for the day, why shouldn't she go home? Slip in extras because she finished half an hour before she normally does and next time she will stretch out the work to the time available.

In fact, put out a list of work you want done while you are away at work or out shopping or whatever and you'll only excite resentment and create an urge to sabotage you and your household. Regular dailies know what has to be done and, given the tools for the job, are best left to get on with it. Like everybody else, they too like to have some discretion in what they do and the way that they do it. If your boss stood over you every minute of the day, you'd soon react, and why this should be unacceptable when it happens to you but not when you do it to somebody else is one of (your) life's little mysteries.

Of course, somebody new in your employment is a slightly different case to somebody who has worked for you for years. You do not know whether the person you hire is as professional as you expect them to be until you have seen what work they do, and how they do it. There is more than one sloppy way to do a job. If they are in the habit of cutting corners – literally sweeping things under the carpet instead of into the bin – you have a right to require them to do the job properly.

There is no doubt, even with the best of dailies, that an occasional discussion on how you want jobs done is an essential aspect of your relationship with them. You can tell them that you do not want them to skimp on the jobs you expect them to do. If you see something completely wrong and unacceptable, you should tell them this, and firmly.

Their bad habits need not be the way they want to do the job; it could just as easily be the way their previous employer let them do it. But you should only need to tell or show them your disapproval once, and, just in case it's your ideas about how to do a job that are eccentric, you could open the discussion by asking them why they did it their way and check that your way has advantages.

Experience shows that dailies left alone often do little extras that they see need doing. They only ignore the obvious extras when you stuff lists of tasks down their throats on arrival each morning – after all, if it's not on your list, Mrs Smarty Pants, you obviously don't want it done, and what good fun it is if the 'extra' is absolutely essential but you've missed it!

The fear that, in your absence, your daily is doing nothing, or not enough, is self-destructive. People who think their dailies are cheating and take counter-measures to prevent it, soon teach their dailies to cheat. Distrust breeds its own fulfilment, and it's always entertaining for the help to think up ways of getting back amidst the boredom of housework.

Au pairs present a special set of management problems. They are invariably younger than regular dailies, and they have an even lower resentment threshold. They have also been known to get involved in *au père* scenes (even *au fils*).

As with your daily, expect too much from them by way of help with the children, or domestic drudgery, and you'll be disappointed. They don't have high levels of enthusiasm for tedious and interminable activity; they also get into teen-ager moods every bit as perplexing as those of your own children.

As with children, establish with a potential au pair the working norm you are looking for, secure their agreement and leave them alone at all other times. If on occasion you need extra help from them, be prepared to reward it in addition to their normal remuneration (though don't offer to do so with too much enthu-siasm too early in your request for their help – it'll only escalate their expectations on other occasions). They, too, will want to vary the work you have set for them in a particular week – they may want to see friends, especially of a romantic nature – and you can negotiate with them about this. Agree on this before they take the time off, rather than afterwards.

Failures to turn up on time for the kids at school, or on a night when you have a dinner engagement, are subject to the usual response of a Superdealer: don't just state your grievance (i.e.

show them how angry you are with them), propose a remedy (what do you want done about it?).

Because somebody works for you in your home does not give you extra rights over them, nor does it imply that somehow they are less worthy of respect than someone who works for you in a garage, a restaurant or an office. A certain familiarity can develop with people who enter your home, and this can be a worthwhile experience for those concerned, but the domestic is worthy, and not just for her hire. She is a person in her own right, doing a job she should know how to do (she does it for herself too) and she is at her best when you avoid implying that she must put up with behaviour that you wouldn't expect for a moment from your colleagues at work, or from other members of the family.

Superdealers concentrate on their objective – a functioning household and family – and leave the professionals (domestic, gardener or au pair, etc.) alone to help them achieve it.

Coping with the world's best negotiators

Children think everything they want costs nothing, and their parents are the only obstacle to them getting it. Hence, they make demands, incessantly – and their parents give in, regularly.

All parents know how to bring up children; not their own, mind you, those of other people! You never fail to meet an expert on how to handle a difficult child in a supermarket, bus queue, beach party or doctor's waiting room, particularly when the noisy brat is somebody else's. But you seldom meet a parent who satisfactorily handles their own kids in a similar situation.

Children are among the world's best manipulative negotiators, and understanding why this is so teaches you something about manipulative negotiation and about children, including your own.

In the world of the child, the parent is the bottomless pit. All their needs are supplied 'free' – food, clothing, warmth, shelter, companionship, entertainment, love, support and access to a television set (or a stereo by the time they are twelve). Those who are waited upon hand and foot are difficult taskmasters. At the slightest slip in service, they throw a tantrum. They also throw a tantrum when things are going fine, just in case the parents forget they are there. Children are only quiet when they are doing something they oughtn't; they only make a noise while being 'good'.

The strength of children as negotiators lies in the asymmetry of values between them and their parents. They learn quickly what adults want most, and they threaten to disturb or withdraw this in order to get what they want (which, by definition, is of high value to them and of low value to the parents; hence parents quickly give in). Parents who want peace and quiet suffer noise and disturbance until the child's demands are met (a glass of squash, a sweet, an extra hour's play before bedtime, etc.). Parents watching television are distracted by their children until they give in; parents easily embarrassed in public are treated to a public temper tantrum that can only be bought off with ice cream, chocolate, toys or such like. In short, children know when to press their demands and are not restrained in their use of sanctions. It's a form of inter-generational terrorism.

True, all parents fight back some of the time, and some parents fight back most of the time. They impose sanctions on the child, or threaten to do so: 'Any more of that and you'll go straight to bed/won't go to the pictures/won't see Santa Claus/won't have your pals round.' Often the threatened sanction is unrealistic ('If you don't stop that, we'll send you home and we'll have a holiday without you'), but only the very young child is intimidated into line by such fantasies. By the time children are old enough to recognise unrealistic threats, they've escalated their demands and the adults are cowed into seeking the quiet life.

Consider what happened the last time you had a negotiation with a child, using threats of sanctions, over something like the ratio of ice cream to cabbage at dinner-time (you prefer the child to eat a lot of cabbage before it gets the ice cream; the brat prefers not to eat any cabbage at all):

'If you don't eat your cabbage, you won't get any ice cream.'

LATER: 'If you don't eat most of that cabbage, you won't get any ice cream.'

All threats about the ice cream have no effect other than to make the child even less inclined to eat cabbage. You get angry about this – perhaps half-heartedly supported by your partner, though more likely they indicate by look or grimace that they think you're making too much of a fuss. This, of course, the child notices: they never miss a hint of a crack in the parental coalition, and they are experts at exploiting one. Later:

'Eat three more spoonfuls of cabbage and you'll get the ice cream.'

and finally:

'OK, eat this one tiny piece and you can have ice cream plus chocolate sauce.'

The postage stamp of cabbage leaf might be half-eaten, painfully as if you are poisoning them, at which point you give in, hand over the ice cream and blame your partner as the original source of the child's conduct.

Your weakness is that you do not have the patience, nor the heart, for a long war of attrition with your children over what are essentially minor matters for you. The child is not so restrained. To him or her, there is a distinct and important difference between the tastes of cabbage and ice cream. It matters to them which they eat. They have their real interests at heart. In fact, they are prepared to suffer and to fight you hard for what they perceive to be a fundamental matter of life and death: cabbage – *ugh!* ice cream – *ahh!* You're not so ambitious, hence you give in.

Some parents surrender early on in their parenthood. The kids do just what they like. The adults give up worrying about the weird and random preferences of the children, and they are oblivious to what the rest of the world thinks of them for doing so. Whether children are happier for being constantly restrained or being totally unfettered is the subject of considerable interest at meetings of Parents Anonymous. No conclusions have been, nor indeed can be, drawn from these discussions (even refugees from Parents Anonymous haven't got an answer).

The world's best negotiators have their parents on the run, whatever they do, and you are only saved from being taken over by your children because time passes and they grow up, and learn to compromise like everybody else.

Is there a Superdeal strategy for dealing with kids? Sure there is, but you had better be warned right now: even the Superdeal strategy only slows down the slide towards your children's first demands!

Successful negotiating with children is directly dependent

upon the amount of time and energy you have available for them.

The less time you have, whether by circumstance or inclination, the more likely your negotiating style alternates between buying peace (i.e. giving in) or refusing to concede anything (i.e. a parental temper tantrum). As children, and other negotiators, appreciate consistency more than they do randomly decided offers, the 'yes, never' style of the parent in a hurry creates more trouble than it's worth and you have time to handle.

Decide what is at stake. Is it an issue of parental authority? If parental authority is important in this case, you may have to spend a lot of time and energy reasserting it, assuming it is being seriously challenged by the child and is not just an excuse on your part to assert it.

If at first you resist a child's demand and then give in when the tantrum becomes unbearable, you teach the child the duration of a tantrum that will get you to give in. Extend the time before your surrender each time, and you simply extend the time you have to endure the next tantrum.

During the tantrum, you are forced to review the importance of the dispute you are trying to win – that is the purpose of the tantrum – and it is here that cracks in the alliance between parents, and unhelpful intervention by grandparents, undermine your determination. Grandparents, for instance, are notorious for criticising 'lack of discipline' in their grandchildren and at the same time sabotaging all attempts to impose any. The child is under no such pressure to review its demands, until exhaustion intrudes, and it has a singlemindedness about gaining its ends that would shame a militant extremist.

Childrens' demands do not always, nor even mainly, challenge parental authority, except in the sense that they are not inclined to take 'no' for an answer. In deciding the significance of what is at stake, consider the very real possibility that the child's demands are perfectly reasonable and that it is only your lethargy, lack of interest, arbitrary mood or sheer bloodymindedness that leads you to say 'no' in the first place. In which case, a war of attrition is hardly justified.

Superdealers improve their negotiating score with children by only contesting issues that they have decided, after careful thought, to be of importance.

Upsetting yourselves and your children for trivial ends is no way to assist a child's journey to adulthood. You must distinguish between a child's demand that is merely inconvenient for you (the wrong time, the wrong place, the wrong sequence of events, etc.), and the demand that is against the interests of the child to obtain.

Tired parents give in to demands they find inconvenient when the child imposes further inconvenience on them (tears, etc.). They might as well have said 'yes' to start with. Demands that are against the child's interest (riding bicycles in traffic, eating too much stodge, having unlimited access to cash, wandering the streets after hours, playing with electrical apparatus, climbing dangerous pylons, etc.) can be resisted, starting with persuasion and running through to meaningful sanctions. Parental resistance to such demands educates the child to distinguish between acceptable and unacceptable lifestyles, assuming that the list of unacceptable demands – those that the parent presumes are against the child's own interests – is highly selective and not virtually universal.

Newborn babies are totally dependent on their parents; young children do a few things for themselves. Teenagers, however, often lapse into total dependence by choice – that is, they neither look after themselves (or their rooms) nor do they help in the household. They avoid housework with a passion similar to that which they reserve for 'pop' idols. The home becomes a hotel, and their parents and other kids are treated as mere servants whose only role in life is to service those of their needs that are not being fulfilled elsewhere.

Superdealers introduce the concept of a mutual obligation to contribute to the work of the household from an early age by requiring a minimum of effort by everybody.

While parents undertake the bulk of the domestic chores, all children are encouraged to do something (set and clear the table, do the dishes, tidy up the communal areas, etc.). Such tasks are related to communal services (everybody benefits from their being done), and they are more appropriate for educating children in mutual obligations than tasks that are purely related to the personal comfort of the parents. Perpetually sending the kids on personal errands – bring my slippers, find the newspaper, change the television channel, bring me a drink, etc. – is unlikely to instil an acceptance of the need to contribute to the household chores.

Children are less likely to appreciate that their parents are not personal servants if they have spent several years in that role themselves, and when they are in the flush of adolescence, they become confident enough to say 'no', or something worse. Parents who object to being treated as skivvies by their teenage children deserve (and receive) a tirade on hypocrisy if their children were never shown by example the difference between *family* as opposed to *personal* service.

Basic household services from which everybody gains should not be directly rewarded. By sharing the work from which everybody gains, nobody directly benefits, except in the sense that the household is less burdensome to run, and is a pleasanter place to be in. Extra services, particularly tasks that are normally done by the parents (washing the car, digging the garden, shopping), can be rewarded, and the extent of the reward can be negotiated. Where personal services are concerned, if the child undertaking the service gains from doing so, they can search (and experience suggests that they do so with alacrity when they want something in the gift of a parent) for other tasks they can undertake in pursuit of additional rewards.

Naturally, the scope for undertaking rewardable tasks, in addition to those communal ones that are expected from them, increases as the child approaches young adulthood. At precisely the same time as the 'troublesome teenager' discovers a distaste for contributing anything to the household, the reward system for doing so gives them more ways to take advantage of their wider abilities and accomplishments.

Superdealers do not force hard bargains on kids who want to undertake a task that is within their competence ('wash the dishes for six months for £2.00'); they negotiate a reward that is generous in amount in order to encourage the acceptance of the principle that you get more out of a household (or any other institution, including waged employment and business) by putting more in.

It is not easy being a parent, nor is it all that easy being a child, but it is a lot easier if an effort is made to encourage involvement by the entire family in the necessary work of the household.

Never was it more truly said that, in the parental relationship with children, 'you can't win 'em all'. Parents give children advice they never took themselves, but they have many opportunities to demonstrate that members of a family can win more by co-operation and negotiation than by the alternatives.

Lovers

While it is true that there is no accounting for taste in human relationships (of the intimate kind), this in itself is no reason not to have any. With billions of people on the planet at any one time (more each day!), it is amazing how often people stick to a bad scene long after it has got worse. It is not as if there is nobody else available who could light your fire and soothe your brow, or whatever it is that you seek from another human being.

With such an abundance of choice, there is no need for anybody (other than those who wish to do so) to accept what somebody else decides is good for them in their personal life. In every case, there is a Superdeal possible, which will either change the relationship for the better, or permit you to search for a better relationship. Hasty and regrettable choices of lovers can be coped with, and replaced with better (or, at least, different) choices.

Lovers negotiate or go under. In fact, affairs usually start with a negotiation, however informally, of a personal 'contract'. These cover acceptable behaviour, expected or offered, and the status of any property brought to or acquired during the relationship. They might be expressed in informal commitments, often, though not always, well sprinkled with romantic gibberish (and not just in the very young!), and sometimes in formal commitments (marriage, for example). Both kinds of commitment can end up being sorted out in a courtroom – a lucrative business for divorce lawyers – which could be avoided if the parties had been more specific, less lighthearted, from the start.

Superdealers recognise that there is a personal contract between lovers and they pay attention to what goes into it. This apparent coolness in no way disqualifies them from the joys of love; it's just that Superdealers keep their heads when all around they see the wreckages of those lovers who didn't.

Many breakdowns in relationships occur either because there was no mutually agreed contract to begin with (the partners

glided into their affair under other, stronger urges and in-
fluences), or in the case where some sort of contract or understanding did exist, one or both the partners changed their
behaviour through time (perhaps they changed their minds).
Good intentions, for example, often fail to keep up with latent
inclinations.

Superdealers know what to include in their contracts, and they
pay close attention to what they are getting into, and with whom.
They never settle for less than the lifestyles they can live with,
and they *trade* for the things they want from the other person
against the things they don't want.

What should be in the contract? That, like the house you live in,
is a matter of personal choice and inclination. And if you get your
contract down to ten rules only, but adultery stays in, you had
better make sure you live close to it, otherwise your partner
makes life miserable for you both, and the relationship falls apart.

*The time to negotiate your personal contract with somebody is
before rather than during the relationship.*

Superdealers know, usually from experience, what they want
from others and what they have available to share with them.

As before, think through what you want, preferably when you
are not sexually aroused. Apply the hooker's principle: things are
valued more before they are supplied than they are afterwards. In
short, arrive at agreement on the terms of your affair before it
begins. Trying to change a relationship after it starts is extremely
difficult. People are less willing to renegotiate their contracts
when they like the ones they have, or think they have.

If your lifestyle requires on occasion that you wind down in a
wine bar till 2 am, it is better (from a negotiating point of view)
that this is acceptable to your lover before they wonder what you
are up to – whether the affair is in its death throes – now that
you've started coming home late. If your needs are not acceptable
to them (why not?), you need to know this before you commit
yourself.

Separate holidays, indeed any absences from home, take a little
longer to accept if they are introduced at a time when your
partner has other expectations. Likewise, unilateral decisions to
have, or not to have, children are difficult to sell to an unwilling
partner who has a different preference.

You might as well put all your own friends – especially those you expect to continue to see and have fun with – on to the agenda for acceptance by your intended partner. Including ex-lovers in your list may be a trifle difficult to win agreement upon, though that is no reason why you shouldn't try if they are important to you. A refusal to accept your friends raises the price of your relationship and, as with any other price, if it's too high, don't buy. Your partner's choice of friends has to be accommodated too, so there is scope for a trade off between the mutually obnoxious!

In sum, communication of preferences, intentions and changes in same is an essential basis of a Superdeal partnership contract. So communicate now; don't hope for it to be reconciled later.

Which phase are you in?

All affairs go through three main phases: *pass, play* and *part*. To do better than average, learn to recognise which phase you are in. Each phase has its own characteristics and requires different skills and techniques. If you are not sure what is going on at any one moment, you could be parting when you should be playing, or passing when you should be 'slipping into something more comfortable'.

There are two kinds of *passes*: those you welcome and those you don't. The latter type are more common than the former. The pass is the first move and, in many cases, the last one, too. For nobody ever got into an affair without making or responding to a pass – though many make passes and don't get into an affair!

Whether it is a chance meeting or a longer association, you do not need to take a pass any further, any more than you have to buy what somebody is selling. In fact, the pass is closely akin to a sales pitch and it is instantly recognisable as such. Superdealers know how to handle sellers and their attempted passes.

When you get a signal, you can respond positively (to encourage the signaller) or negatively (to discourage them) or you can ignore it (though don't bet that ignoring a pass curbs the other party's ambitions – their persistence is in inverse proportion to their attractiveness).

Passes come in all manner of styles and with varying degrees of bluntness. They can be solitary one-offs, simple try-ons or part of highly complex game-plans.The trouble with solitary one-offs is that they may be missed (accidentally or intentionally) and hence you signal more avidly, until, if not careful, you are signalling like HMS *Victory* at Trafalgar. The less subtle the signal, the more embarrassing it is to be turned down. A try-on that can be seen coming six miles away will not woo somebody who prefers the subtle approach. A corny try-on is so off-putting that only un-interesting people use them – B movie scriptwriters have a lot to answer for.

Some people live for the chase, love the moves and get as much fun working out a strategy for their game-plan as they do when, or if, they achieve their goal. But don't underestimate the attraction of two people 'playing games' with each other. A mild flirtation, like a mild libation, can be a challenge to one's good intentions.

The pass has a billion variants, depending on the interests, habits and (hopefully) the willing gullibility of the hearer. The classic pass can take the form of:

Passer: I haven't heard decent music for weeks.
Passee: Nor me. I can't bear the stuff they call popular today.

If you're interested or tempted, or both, pick up the signal and respond:

Passer: Do you like traditional or modern jazz?
Passee: Both. As long as it's played on stereo.
Passer: I've got a large collection of jazz at my flat, and a stereo system. Would you care to join me?

From here on, it's game, set and match, *if the parties wish to play.*
   Passes are more likely when you:

– have been eating, drinking or socialising.
– are unaccompanied.
– have discovered (or invented!) a common interest.
– are visibly not getting on with your partner.
– announce that you are bored with your life, career, spouse and/or prospects.
– need something that the other person can give.
– have to be somewhere else in five minutes.

   People spend a small fortune on making themselves more

attractive to other people. In marketing, they call it packaging. It's no good being similar: if you look and sound the same, your heart's desire might as well stay with the one they've got already. Hence, be different, or appear to be so.

Switch-selling is a classic move in both business and *affaires de coeur*, with the difference that in business the seller tries to switch from the cheap to the expensive, while in the affair, the seller switches you down from expensive or exotic promises to the cheaper, though hopefully not nasty reality. If she'd love to go with you to Maxim's in Paris, she'll go to Le Caveaux in the King's Road; if he agrees to visit California with you next year, then he'll accept a wild weekend in Sheffield (which may mean he never gets to California!).

How to play

In the *play* phase, there is a risk of one last great switch sale: what you get is not what you wanted, or having wanted it, you now want something different.

People are extremely difficult to deal with. Individuals have lives of their own; their views, hopes and behaviours are not always acceptable to us. Nowhere is this more true than when people live together. The hellish irritations of other people – which Sartre thought was best represented by three people condemned for ever to sit in the same room – can blow up into dramas and crises of unimaginable grief to all concerned. Lovers have no special protection from the irritations of each other as people. A lovers' tiff or a *crime passionnel* are no less awesome than a quarrel between neighbours or a drunken knifing outside the local pub.

Superdealers can reduce the traumas of personal relationships, though nobody can ever quite eliminate them. They do this by understanding the processes by which a minor irritation blows up into a major conflict and confrontation, and take the necessary measures to cool the tension and resolve the problem.

Consider the case of the man who wants to go to a golf tournament and the woman who wants him to take the kids to the beach. No doubt you can think of all kinds of ways of accommodating the wishes of each party without greatly upsetting the basis of their relationship. But that is because you have not been given much detail about the conflicting timings, the presentation of the alternative activities, and the tensions underlying each partner's wish that the other should do what they want them to do. Also, and most importantly, you are not involved. You are an outsider who brings nothing to the debate that can contaminate it with tension. You take a more objective view about what options are available and how the parties might be reconciled. Being more objective, you are at once more pleased with yourself for being so much smarter than the people who are lining up for a ding-dong row about the proposed whereabouts of Dad and the kids on Saturday.

Take the emotional tension out of a relationship and you don't have a relationship; put it back in and you have the basis of an emotionally tense agenda.

Courts have long got used to the fact that people who see the same event (a car smash, a punch-up, a robbery), even under the intimidation of swearing to tell the truth, the whole truth and nothing but the truth, often appear to have been present at different events, so much at variance are their versions of what they think actually happened. Crowds at football matches divide into those who think it was a goal kick and the other lot who think it was a penalty.

Partners are no less vulnerable to selective interpretation of the same events or behaviour. If they think they are being 'neglected', then any behaviour, including the most unlikely, can be shown to prove their predisposition to feelings of neglect. The mere recounting of the 'evidence' each has to prove their views can itself lead to a storm of indignant protest or to sarcasm.

Superdealers are wary of drawing conclusions on the basis of the 'evidence' of events or behaviour.

They seek another explanation and, when appropriate, ask for one, and they think carefully about what they are told, preferring goodwill to suspicion.

The problem of 'double standards' is not confined to particular relationships. It abounds in all aspects of society: rowdy mayhem by young yobbos is merely high spirits if committed by young accountants; your affair was a mere nothing, your spouse's an act worthy of biblical punishment. Double standards are common because they are convenient. They conform to our prejudices and are wonderful rationalisations for just about any inconsistency in our system of personal beliefs.

Superdealers search for consistent criteria by which to judge their own and their partner's behaviour.

The mere act of trying to define criteria often produces an acceptable single standard by which behaviour can be put into context and purged of emotional connotations.

Under emotional stress, it is common to go to an extreme position rapidly. This way we make a major problem out of not seeing the minor problem. Crisis management consists of containing the problem to specific issues, not going to nuclear war in one leap.

The guy at the front desk refuses to do anything about his company's incompetence: you storm out vowing never to do business with them again (you were talking to the wrong guy in the organisation). Your spouse doesn't understand your concerns about another Christmas with mother-in-law: you demand a divorce (you hope to win with threats what you lost with persuasion – try negotiating). You ask your kids to clear away their toys: they go into tantrums that threaten to waken the dead (have they negotiated with you before?).

Superdealers don't go to extreme positions in a hurry, if at all, but instead widen the range of their options when faced with a difficult or slow-moving deadlock.

Superdealers decide first what problem they think they have and they examine the alternatives that are available and which might be satisfactory to both parties. Then they present their version of the problem to their partner and ask for comments. If the temperature rises (as it almost certainly will), they stay cool and ask neutral questions, and seek to elicit an alternative from them. They settle for the best deal they can get, which might be short of, or different from, the deal they first proposed. They avoid winning at the expense of their partner, preferring *something* to the bleakness of *nothing*.

If every little issue blows up into a major confrontation (unless you enjoy the dramatic school of domestic bliss), there is something wrong, or about to go wrong, with the relationship. There is no point in permanent unhappiness or permanent distress. It's time, perhaps, for a long chat with your partner in which you listen a great deal more than you talk. Think about what they tell you and work out what you want before you respond.

Salvage, at sea and in the home, is hard work.

'I SEE HE'S TAKEN HIS HALF OF THE HOUSE.'

How to negotiate a divorce
Parting is sometimes the least worst of the decisions you can make when you, or the other person, can no longer provide what you both want out of your short lives (pubs, wine bars, doctors' surgeries and the courts are full of the consequences of worse decisions).

Divorce, like the end of a stormy affair, is often traumatic. This is not surprising, as it is a common feature of the parting process that one partner may not be as sold as the other on the idea of a separation as a solution to their problems. Indeed, the trauma is intensified, almost unbearably for a while, when the idea of a separation is introduced by one partner to the complete and utter surprise of the other.

People avoid separation except as a last resort, unless they are the kind who threaten to leave from the first day and do so with monotonous regularity at the slightest provocation. Some refuse to consider separation because of moral, family or religious objections.

Superdealers approach the prospect of separation with the same behaviour as they do any other proposal – that is, with a careful eye on their own interests.

And it's with your interests, not your emotions, you must begin. You might think that the individuals involved in a divorce are the most important considerations for the two parties. This is a mistake. A relationship is important, as are the innocent parties to that relationship (the children, for example), but the road to ruination is built on the misdirected concerns of the parties for how negatively they feel about each other.

A house is not just a home, it's an asset, too. So are the physical things in and around the home. When you break up a home, you do more than separate the people; you disentangle the previously accumulated wealth of the parties and, in the process, often do immense damage to the income-earning capacities of the people who separate. There is a direct connection between poverty and single-parent families (most of them the result of divorces, separations and failed liaisons). Many formerly well-off couples who divorce each other suffer a substantial drop in their living standards as a result. He can't afford to buy a house of the same quality; she can't earn enough to buy a house at all, etc. (including vice versa).

A badly negotiated divorce can go against the longer-term interests of each party, though the emotional fall-out, as immensely damaging as it is myopic, may be so strong as to preclude anything other than a war of attrition, plus some spiteful revenge.

Superdealers rise above the emotional issues (but they don't ignore them) and concentrate their energies on ensuring a survivable living standard for both parties after the divorce. Screwing former lovers to the wall, draining them of every last penny, crushing them with debt, making life bloody miserable and cursing them with a spiteful tongue do not appear in the Superdeal agenda.

If it does in yours, it might be worth a look at what this means for you, and for her/him, a year or so down the track. I won't offer you an illustration: simply call in at the nearest Social Security office and talk to a few 'cases'; for a free cup of coffee and a cigarette, you'll see your future life story in an earlier crop of vengeful lovers.

Far better to negotiate the disposal of the properties held in common by you both. This is where pre-marital recognition of your title to existing property comes in handy. Much better to have sorted out who owns what while you are both in an accommodating mood, than later, when your atrocities have hit the fan, and your spouse is feeling less than best pleased with you and your interests.

If, a long time ago, you had agreed that, in the event of a separation, all common property would be shared on a fifty-fifty basis, or some other mutually convenient formula, then you can apply that agreed formula to the disposal of existing assets. The equity in the house (its selling price minus the mortgage and selling costs) can be divided in any proportions that you mutually agree to. If you are pushing the hardest for the divorce, you can expect a lot of pressure on the size of your share of the equity and which of you should pay the selling costs. Alternatively, 'selling' your share in the equity to your former partner, or 'buying' their share from them, makes sense as it avoids the cost of selling the house to a third party and having less equity to share.

I know that some people get emotional about who gets the house (thinking of it as a public affirmation as to which of you is 'guilty'), and they prefer that nobody gets it, but this is rather silly. Few people give a damn about your domestic arrangements and even fewer 'take sides' in everyday occurrences like divorces. If the house equity is diminished significantly by a public sale, you worsen your economic position by pursuing this route, assuming that the other party is willing to 'buy' your share or 'sell' theirs. Depending on the circumstances, try for a 'buy-out'.

There are some things that you can trade for your share of the house equity. For example, you could 'sell' your equity in full and final settlement of any future financial obligations to the other party. These obligations are worth avoiding if they are likely to cripple your finances and force on you a lower socio-economic lifestyle. In addition, it might be in your interest, when on the receiving end of a 'buy-out' proposal, to get the house valued and judge whether the sum fully meets your own needs.

Other possessions can be divided up on an item-by-item basis. Some are obvious, such as things that go with the house being traded for removables. Two-car families have less of a problem than one-car families, but it is hardly worth fighting over a popular car that is replaceable at no great expense (with Mercedes and other expensive motors, common sense can be confused with self-image, and not enough consideration about their value).

The general principle followed by Superdealers is to arrange the break-up of the relationship with the least damage to each party's future socio-economic position.

Unless that is an agreed objective, the consequences are unattractive.

If somebody wants you to change what you had expected to be a more or less permanent relationship, you have negotiating strengths unmatched by the other person. People who want out in a hurry are like buyers who must have what you are selling – they make concessions quicker than they would otherwise.

Superdealers use their strengths to protect their interests, not to damage them by indulging their emotions.

Faced with demands for a divorce, carefully consider your best interests, and these must start from an equitable division of the spoils of the relationship. Embarking on a wasting war of attrition, no matter what your initial strengths, or how upset you feel about it all, could drive the object of your bile into a 'scorched hearth' counter-attack, and you'll both end up poorer (lawyers just love families that break up and fight dirty), which isn't very smart, is it?

11

How to acquire money

You can acquire money in one of five ways:
– inherit it.
– earn it.
– marry into it.
– steal it.
– borrow it.

While the meek may (eventually) inherit the earth, few of us inherit its wealth. In fact, relying on inheritance to acquire money is like gambling for it – the odds are stacked against you (which is why you'll never meet a poor bookie). Perhaps one day you'll qualify for a windfall inheritance. Somebody might take a fancy to you and leave you their wealth – but then they might just fancy you . . . and give it to somebody else.

You can acquire money by earning it. Having a regular job is highly regarded by most people – more highly by those who haven't got one, less so by those ground down by steady work for steady pay. But earning money by working is a slow way to get rich. In fact, if you have to put in a lot of effort to get a small wage, you are more likely to end up poorer than you want to be. Even if your job pays you well for doing very little, you are more likely to become a bored retiree rather than rich and young enough to enjoy it.

In addition to inheriting it and working for it, you could hope to marry into money. But relying on marrying money adds the vagaries of judgement (hers, or his, not yours) to your already slim chances of inheritance. And if you think you won't have to work for it having married it (there is a limit to how often you can shut your eyes, and mouth, and count your blessings), you've obviously inherited nothing but a poor sense of judgement so far.

Stealing money is an alternative. It is not recommended, however, unless you are very good at it, have no conscience, and do not mind being resident from time to time (and perhaps longer) in one of Her Majesty's prisons.

This leaves borrowing as the potential road to riches. And believe me, it is! More has been done on borrowed money than was ever done on earned income, inheritance and theft combined. Columbus, for example, didn't discover America in the *Santa Maria* off his own back; he did it on borrowed money. Neil Armstrong's 'giant step for mankind' was possible only because of NASA's giant borrowing of said mankind's money.

Little that is really expensive is bought with your own money. How many houses in your district are bought by people without mortgages? If the answer is more than 10 per cent, the houses must be very cheap, in which case you are living in the wrong district or your neighbours are flush with cash, in which case they are the very people who can make you richer.

You don't have to live next to richer people to use their money, nor do you need to know the people from whom you borrow, though they may want to know something about you! Most people who lend money are actually of quite modest means, though they tend to be represented by people who know what they are doing (bank or building society managers, and smoothies from the finance companies) because they are well organised. When you want to borrow money, especially large amounts, you had better get yourself organised too.

Of the five main ways of acquiring money, only two (earning or borrowing it) are realistic; the others are fanciful (inheriting, marrying or stealing it). You need a Superdeal strategy to maximise your potential spending power, both from the money you earn from your employment and the money you are able to borrow. You can use your salary, by borrowing against it, to raise your capital, and you can use your capital, through profit, rent and interest on it, to increase your spending. And the beauty about the *Superdeal* strategy is that it is open to anyone – no matter what their current circumstances, what the limits of their ambitions, what the inhibitions in their personal make-up, or what they value in their lives – to apply the strategy to their incomes, or lack thereof. Within a short period they will have demonstrable evidence that they are getting more out of their incomes than they were before.

First, you must find out how well or badly you are doing to date. For this you need to find out your net worth.

What are you worth?

A cynic, said Oscar Wilde, knows the price of everything and the value of nothing. There are a lot of cynics about because few people know what they are worth. Not knowing what you are worth is like not knowing your sex – it gets confusing when it matters!

Now it is a fact that income and wealth are not equally distributed, not even in those societies dedicated to the principle that they ought to be. And even if they were equally distributed, you would still face the same problem of making what you have go further – and to make what you have go further, it helps to know how much you have.

What do you own? If you are not too sure, ask yourself: if I fell under a bus today, what would be left after all my debts were paid?

You might object to assessing what you are worth because your worth as a person cannot be measured – 'human life and spirit are invaluable', etc. True, but you are not measuring your worth in the sight of your Maker – nor how you value yourself in sight of a mirror. Human worth is truly incalculable, and the world would indeed be spiritually poorer if our worth were not recognised in this sense. Your monetary worth, however, represents the difference between what you *own* and what you *owe* at any one moment (known as your *net worth* because you deduct what you owe from what you own).

The pound coin in your pocket entitles you to a pound's worth of goods and services, presently in the possession of other people, all just as worthy as you, and just as determined to hold on to what they have until you pay them for letting you have what you want. Think how you would react to a stranger expecting to be able to purchase your car for nothing but a sense of their human warmth! Your worth is a measure of your entitlement, or capacity, to consume the goods and services owned by other people. If you are worth a lot, you have a greater capacity to consume than if you are worth a little.

Your annual income from employment is not part of your net worth. If you died today, your employment income would cease immediately. It would not be counted into your estate (other than any part of it unpaid before your demise – after the tax man had taken his due!). What you might have earned over the next twelve months, or for the rest of your working life, is not relevant to what you are worth today.

Any cash that you have to hand – perhaps from your last pay cheque – is, of course, included in your net worth because it is available for distribution to the beneficiaries of your estate. Similarly with future incomes from investments, interest on bank or building society deposits, any rents from property you own and dividends from shares. The assets that provide you with these incomes are included in your net worth, either by the actual amount on deposit in the bank or building society, or by the amount your assets can be sold for.

A Chattels and Debts table (*see* p. 184) helps you summarise your net worth. Fill in the relevant information about your financial position as things stand today, then draw up similar tables – ones more suited to your circumstances – at future dates to see if your monetary worth is improving (Superdeal!) or getting worse as time goes by. Enter in the approximate value of your assets, beginning with your place of abode. There is no need to undertake a professional valuation; an estimate is sufficient.

No property – house or otherwise – is worth more than what somebody is prepared to pay for it, and this is nowhere more true than when you come to value the contents of your home. Unless you own antiques of an easily determined minimum value, the worth of your house contents is unlikely to be easy to estimate. If your household contents were to come under an auctioneer's hammer, what would they be likely to fetch?

That you will swing between under- and over-valuation is a safe assumption, though you are going to be better off in the long run if you under- rather than over-value what you possess. Delusions of grandeur in the value of one's material possessions are less useful than the same in personal deportment. Your net worth has nothing to do with what it would cost to replace your house contents – it's about what they are worth to possible buyers. Hence, be conservative about their valuation, but even if you are, you may still be surprised as to just how much your house contents are worth.

Cars, caravans, boats, etc. have active second-hand markets that will give you an idea of the value of the ones you own. Second-houses, holiday chalets, timeshare weeks and such like can be valued approximately from the prices realised in the markets that sell them.

Cash is valued at its unit of account – a hundred pounds in the bank is worth a hundred pounds – and your bonds and shares have market values that are published in the newspapers. Insurance entitlements often cause a problem, it being a fact of life that most people are ignorant of exactly what their life assurance or pension fund entitlement is at any particular time. Ask whoever takes the cash for your insurances what exactly they are worth if you dropped dead today (assure them that you have no immediate intention of so doing, which, no doubt, will provoke them to try to sell you more insurance!).

Add up the Chattels (assets) column and enter it at the foot of the table, and turn to the Debts column. Here the rule is the opposite of the advice for valuing your assets – instead of being conservative, be liberal. If you understate your assets and overstate your debts, you are less likely to be misled into a false sense of security – and the fright might do you good. Note also that, whereas the value of the things we own tends to be shrouded in uncertainty, the amounts we owe to other people are always specific. Lenders who don't know the exact amounts they are owed soon cease to be able to lend anything to anybody.

The amount of your outstanding mortgage and any other loans on your property (home improvement loans, for example) are obtainable from a recent statement from your bank or building society. Hire-purchase debts are obtainable directly from the accounts sent to you by the lenders. Likewise with your overdraft(s), and unpaid bills, such as gas, electricity, telephone, rates, other fuels, food, school fees, garage and household repairs (and don't forget the outstanding balances on your credit cards!).

CHATTELS AND DEBTS TABLE

I own:	Current value £	I owe:	Outstanding debt £
House/flat	....	Mortgage(s)	....
Contents		Home loans	....
carpets	....	HP, etc.	....
curtains	....		....
electricals	....		....
furniture	....		....
valuables	....		....
Car(s)	....	Car, boat loans	....
Caravan	....		....
Boat(s)	....		....
2nd house(s)	....		....
Contents	....		....
Timeshare	....		....
Contents	....		....
Savings			
Bank accounts	....	Overdrafts	....
Building soc.	....		....
Other	....	Tax debts	....
Investments		Other	....
Bonds	....	Monies owed	....
Loans	....	to traders	....
Shares	....	Other unpaid	
Insurance		bills	....
Life	....		....
Mortgage	....		....
Pension	....	Credit	
Other	....	cards	....
Cash	....		....
TOTAL ASSETS	£	TOTAL DEBTS	£

Deducing my DEBTS from my ASSETS
I AM WORTH £ _____ Date: ....

Add up the Debts column and enter it at the foot of the table. Now deduct the (hopefully) smaller Debts total from the (hopefully) larger Chattels total. The result is your *net worth*. Enter this sum at the bottom of the table and write in the date, for whether this is big or small (or even negative), this is the number that you will be looking to increase (positively!) over the next few years.

As a rough short-term guide, you aim to have a positive net worth that is about ten times your income. Hence, if you have an income from all sources of £20,000 you are doing fine if your net worth is about £200,000, i.e. your assets exceed your debts by £200,000. If all else came to nought, and you could earn the interest off your assets, you would be able to earn sufficient to cover your current income of £20,000. In effect, you would not be getting any richer but (ignoring inflation) you would not be on the poverty line.

Your longer-term aim is to push up your net worth to twenty or more times your earnings. Each year you can trace your progress, or otherwise, by calculating your net worth from the table.

If your present net worth is less than ten times your earnings, you should aim to increase it in stages towards that target. In the case where your net worth is negative (your debts are larger than the sum of your assets), you know just how vulnerable you are to the proverbial slings and arrows. Loss of your earning capacity for any reason would throw you down the socio-economic scale and you need, therefore, a strategy to reverse that balance.

The conclusion is clear (and compelling): succeed in increasing your net worth and you will become richer; if you don't, you won't. It's as simple as that!

How to borrow money

Contrary to their image, banks like to lend money. If they didn't lend money, they'd go out of business. The ogre of a manager sitting across the desk from you is actually desperately keen to find somebody to lend money to, for without a customer who borrows, there is absolutely no point in him having clients who lend.

HONEYSETT.

Debt, therefore, is not a burden, it's an opportunity, at least to a Superdealer. Only those who believe that borrowed money pays for a dissolute lifestyle see getting into debt as a threat to common sense. Such people, and there are plenty of them, believe that if you lend anybody money, you can't pretend that you don't know what they want it for, which makes you as guilty as you believe they intend to be. They also believe the opposite side of the coin: if you borrow money from somebody else, they will know what you want it for, which makes you feel as guilty as they think you are. Against the prejudices of the sanctimonious, even the Lord battles in vain.

Of course, if you borrow money merely to extend your consumption, then you could certainly end up stony broke, for sooner or later the interest payments on the money you previously borrowed eat up all your income, and you cannot pay back the amount you owe. At this point, the credit card companies require you to return their bits of plastic, your bank manager calls you in for an interview, and you prove once again that a fool with money often ends up without any.

But borrowing to enhance your net worth is not only worthy of the support of bank managers, it is also a worthy activity for those who want to become Superdealers.

Except by inheritance, theft or Scrooge-like penury, nobody gets going without borrowing. The secret of borrowing to get going, as opposed to borrowing to get by, is to use your borrowing power to the full to enhance your net worth – in other words, to become an *efficient* borrower.

Efficient borrowers acquire assets rather than liabilities: the former not only have value in their own right and gain in value over time, but they also contribute to future income; the latter decrease current income, a wholly avoidable expense except in the most dire of circumstances.

Borrowers are dependent upon the whims of another person. Lenders do not have to lend you the money; they can lend it to someone else, and leave you to your own devices.

It is said by some that banks never lend money to people who need it, which is true as far as it goes. If you need money that badly, you are a poor risk, and it is the banker's estimate of how risky it is to lend you money that usually determines whether, or to what extent, the bank makes the loan. Your character – or rather how it is perceived by the lender – is probably the most important determinant in whether you will get a loan. Unfortunately, most borrowers are relatively unknown to potential lenders.

Your lendability is enhanced if you consider a loan a personal obligation to the lender, transcending the legal niceties of the loan arrangements – in other words, you will pay it back come hell or high water.

The building society or bank manager knows next to nothing about you the first time you do business with them – hence, they require that you meet fairly strict conditions. In their phraseology, they lend you money 'subject to status', and they institute a procedure to find out about your status. That is why they ask questions about your current and prospective income, what kind of regular savings record you have, how much you can make as a deposit, and what kind of credit risk you have proven to be in the past with other lenders. If you have only been in a job a few weeks, have changed addresses several times in the past few years, have never saved a bean in your life before, and have outstanding HP debts, plus a record of missed repayments, you cannot expect a banker to be desperately keen to offer you a £30,000 loan.

In banking, failing to lend anybody any money is bad enough, but lending it to just about anybody is suicidal.

Now it does not follow, because of your past debt record, that you will *never* qualify for a substantial loan. You can act now to alter your future creditworthiness. And as you certainly won't qualify for much until you do change your behaviour (and intentions), you should start doing that right now.

A record of job and address changes is more difficult to alter in the short term, but you can begin to establish a regular savings record today. If you don't have a bank savings account, open one this very day and deposit £1 in it, and another £1 every week from now on (more if you can). It's not much but it's a start, and it's the fact of that start that is important because this registers positively in the banker's mind as he or she listens to your request for a large loan.

When lenders ask if you have any outstanding HP or other loan accounts, they are not necessarily assuming that your current debts are too high for them to make a new loan to you. The very fact that others have given you credit in the past is a very big plus factor with new creditors. This view is totally confirmed when you demonstrate that you have *always* met repayment obligations.

Hence, if you cannot meet a repayment on any debt, *it is always better that you inform the creditor immediately* – they are bound to notice that you have missed your repayment – *and make alternative arrangements with them*. The more responsibility that you show here, even for small amounts, the better for you as the years go by. Bad debts, even trivial ones, remain on your credit file – hence, clear them – and establish a long run of 'clean' years that show you have altered your habits even though you occasionally slipped in the past. For example, if you face a short-term problem with a debt, contact the bank and arrange a short-term loan or overdraft *before* the debt is due. You earn 'Brownie' points for doing so and you avoid a blemish on the character record you are trying to establish.

Bank managers are continually shifted around the bank's branches – for one thing, it discourages collusive fraud – but your borrowing records remain for the information of the new manager, and he or she may be less amenable to lending to a poor risk.

In summary, if you have a poor credit record, this reflects on your character as far as the lender is concerned. You may still negotiate the loan that you want, but only on more onerous terms (smaller amount, higher rate of interest, tighter security).

So begin to alter the perceptions of potential lenders about your character right now by altering your behaviour – start saving something regularly if you have no record of regular saving, and from now on meet *all* repayment deadlines, no matter how trivial the amount or, if it is serious, by making suitable arrangements in advance to cover any short-falls with a temporary loan or over-draft.

Lenders are interested in two other things besides your charac-ter. First, your capacity to pay the interest on the loan and, eventually, to pay back the loan itself, and secondly, your pledged security for the loan in case you default.

Some people confuse their ability to make pledges of security against a possible default on the loan with their capacity to pay the loan back. This puts you on the road to ruin if your repayment capacity is in doubt.

The lender requires security, either in the form of title to your property or by way of a personal guarantee, only as a last resort in case you default on the debt. Hence, the fact that you have some property suitable to be pledged as security is not the decisive factor in your decision to go for a loan. You are more interested in the efficiency of your borrowing – what does it permit you to do and continue doing that otherwise would be denied to you?

Borrowing merely to maintain your consumption of goods and services means borrowing for the least efficient of purposes. Living standards that are based on borrowed money are unlikely to improve, except in the very short run, and once the repay-ments bite, your future ability to live within your income dim-inishes, making you progressively worse off. Trying to stave off the day of reckoning by consuming your capital – borrowing against your property – means you lose your capital (putting your net worth into the red) and you still go bust.

Banks seldom make errors of judgement on whom they lend to, and they charge high enough rates of interest on their loans to make a handsome profit on the good debtors and to cover them against any bad ones. Remember that, when you pay back a loan, you are also helping to pay back the loans of those customers who defaulted!

All bank lending rates are negotiable. The manager likes to quote a rate as if it is fixed ('four points over base') and most borrowers meekly assume it to be so. But give him a reason for a lower rate (good security, all the business you do with the bank, long-term benefits all round, the existence of competition for your business, etc.), and he will almost certainly shave the interest charge, even if only by a half-point. Keep in mind that a regular income of, say, £15,000 a year grosses to £600,000 in a forty-year working lifetime, which is good business for a bank and puts you into a strong bargaining position.

Bank prices for money are no different from shop prices for freezers. Most people pay the bank's mark-up so that the latter therefore has room for a preferential deal with you – *but only if you ask for it*. Just because the manager reads off a printed schedule of charges, it does not mean he is tied down to them. Bank managers have discretion – they are promoted on the basis of their discretionary reliability – and you can call upon them to exercise it.

When borrowing money, you are not driven into the arms of a monopoly – banks, building societies and money shops all compete for your custom. It pays to let the manager know that you know what is on offer in the marketplace.

Borrowing enhances your net worth if it is spent on acquiring assets. Which assets you acquire is a personal matter, but property (of the three-bedroomed type in short-term lets in the neater neighbourhoods) has long been a good bet. Luxury cars, yachts and furniture depreciate in value. Antiques, paintings, rare books and some stamps appreciate. Gold is only valuable as a long stop – a collapse in the world economy – and speculative gambits in commodities are only worth the risk if you want rid of your cash surplus. The more you enhance the value of your assets, the more you can realise your ambitions to spend more out of the income they regularly earn, or the appreciation they produce when they are sold.

To become a *Superdeal* borrower, you have to throw off the shackles of merely being a borrower to supplement your income on a short-term basis. A small debt is your problem; a large debt is the bank's problem. The larger the amount you are able to borrow for a net-worth enhancing purpose, the sooner you will be better off.

Many people who borrow money self-select themselves out of going for big amounts and they end up with a lot of hassle for trivial amounts. Perhaps it's because, deep down, they believe that borrowing is slightly immoral, and that they ought not to borrow too much, if they have to borrow anything at all. In short, when it comes down to it, they chicken out of going for what they are fully capable of achieving, and settle, perhaps happily, for less.

Nobody can make you get into more debt than you are willing and able to carry. But by avoiding getting into debt, you may be passing up real, and safe, opportunities for a larger slice of the cake, which is, after all, the best test of whether you deserve the living standards to which you think you are entitled.

Readers of *Superdeal*, and practitioners of its message, should by now be able to contemplate a more robust approach to the spending of their personal incomes and to the creative use of other people's money to enhance their own net worth.

Hence, walk right into that bank manager's office, tell him straight how much you want, and then why you want it. Convince him that you know what you are doing and he will gladly lend you the money. And if he doesn't, leave the bank (it's no worse than dealing with a used-car seller), and go in search of a banker who knows what he's doing, and when you find one, Superdeal him into having your business.

12

Superdeal!

A Superdeal strategy is basically a simple one, so simple in fact that it is amazing how many people are unaware of the power they could have, the income they could save and the personal distress they could avoid if only they applied it.

To Superdeal:

- *Decide* why you want to buy something.
- *Choose* factual not fanciful reasons for having it.
- *Survey* what is on offer.
- *Prioritise* your wants, likes and don't wants.
- Don't *praise* the seller's product.
- *Identify* the price-inclusive offer.
- *Require* a discount.
- *Trade* for add-ons and take-offs.
- *Propose* special deals.
- *Walk away* if the seller refuses to budge.
- *Search* for another seller, or do without the product.

The above applies to buying something, but by now you should be able to revise it for when you are selling and when dealing with a bureaucrat, your spouse or lover, your kids, your neighbour, the daily help or whoever. Keep to the Superdeal strategy when you negotiate about anything and you'll get a better deal than the one that the other guy first proposes.

Superdeals begin with *preparation*. No matter how big or small the issue, decide what it is that you want. Write it down. Be specific. Have as long a list as you like.

Now think about it. Don't claim that you have no time to think. Twenty seconds is a long time (check twenty seconds off your watch right now). Many people take too little time to prepare for a major negotiation – they jump into major confrontations without a blink between the offer and their response.

How much of what you want can you *realistically* expect to get?

To decide, divide your wants into the things that you *want most*, and the others you'd merely *like*. You give up like-to-gets (on this occasion) to get your want-mosts, and to avoid your *don't wants*.

You don't expect to get everything, for if you expect everything, why are you negotiating? The deal is going to fall short of your total wants (true for the other guy, too), hence, answer the question: what among all my wants am I prepared to sacrifice to achieve those things I want most?

Now think about the *variable* versions of your wants.

For example: your want-most, say, is compensation for the effort your boss required of you during an emergency. Compensation comes in variable versions, such as:

– cash
– kind
– time off
– taxi ride home
– promotion
– a mention in the company magazine
– a new office
– an old one redecorated

While compensation of some kind is a want-most, each version has varying values for you (indeed, they have varying values for your boss, and what's most valuable to you may be cheap for her). Large amounts of cash are preferable to small amounts, and if the boss insists that only a small amount is available (out of petty cash), choose to go for something else.

Thinking about what you want, the form that you want it in and how valuable each variable is to you *before* you open negotiations gives you more confidence and more command of the outcome than if you negotiate 'blind'. **Superdealers prefer to be in the driving seat to being driven.**

When you're face to face with the other guy, you are not upset by their refusal to give you all that you want. If (unlikely) they give you everything, you obviously did not ask for enough!

Lower the stress between you by improving your own behaviour. *Do not*:

– interrupt them
– be sarcastic
– shout them down
– get emotional
– accuse them of anything
– attack them
– make threats
– insult them
– question their parentage
– hit them
– walk out

Try instead three Superdeal behaviours:

– listen to what they say
– ask questions about what they say
– summarise what they say

Tell them what you want, and why. Watch their reactions and listen to their responses. Deadlocks occur because of emotional arguments, and arguments occur when you don't listen to what they are saying.

If you don't tell them what you want, you'll never improve on their first offer. So make a *proposal*.

Avoid being too specific with your first proposals. Tell her you want 'compensation', without mentioning how much or in what form; tell him you want changes in his behaviour, without specifying what will happen if he doesn't (divorce, etc.); tell her you cannot accept her offer on the rent, without specifying what higher rent you would take, and so on.

If they want to do a deal, they are bound to ask for more details about what you want: 'how much compensation are you looking for?' 'which specific behaviour of mine is objectionable?' 'what rent are you looking for?' If they don't want to do a deal, they'll argue about generalities, or about attributes of your behaviour. (You know how to handle this with Superdeal behaviour.) But once they start asking questions about your proposals (and you about theirs), a deal is possible, though not necessarily the one either of you first thought of – all deals differ from each side's first demands.

Superdealers never make concessions – they trade them. They bargain one thing for another.

If your kids want to borrow the car, they can wash it first (and, better still, when they get back!); if they want to watch another channel on television during your favourite programme, they can clean up the tool shed, do the shopping and pour you a drink.

To bargain, Superdealers exchange things that they have for things that they want. They tell the other guy the price of agreement: 'You accept my conditions and I will agree to your offer.'

Superdealers value the things they trade in terms of their value to the other party – what may be of no consequence to you (a day off work) may be of immense value to the au pair. Concessions that are cheap for you and that are highly valued by the other guy are the best concessions to trade with – they give you negotiating leverage.

Superdealers know that they sometimes have to walk away from a deal, a person, a scene. You don't have to take what they offer on the only terms they quote. If they won't budge, you will, but not on your reasonable demands: you'll budge out of their lives or their business, and seek a better deal elsewhere.

Open up with 'On the other hand, we could do it this way' and search for that better deal. That way you'll do better more times than you'll do worse.

And that has got to be good for you, your income, your family, your business and your future.

Happy Superdealing!

Index